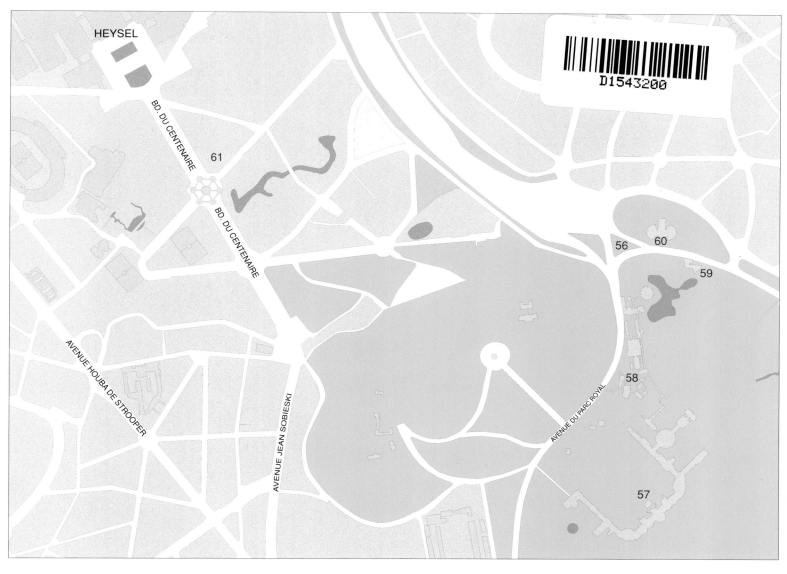

HEYSEL

BD . DU CENTENAIRE

61

BD . DU CENTENAIRE

AVENUE HOUBA DE STROOPER

AVENUE JEAN SOBIESKI

AVENUE DU PARC ROYAL

56   60

59

58

57

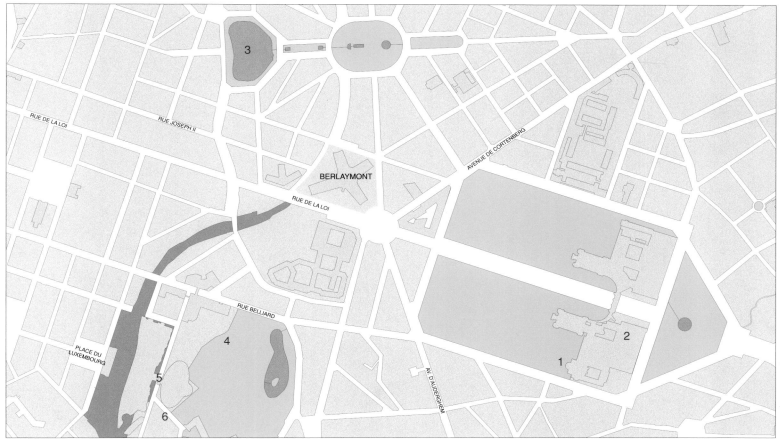

RUE DE LA LOI

RUE JOSEPH II

3

BERLAYMONT

AVENUE DE CORTENBERG

RUE DE LA LOI

RUE BELLIARD

PLACE DU
LUXEMBOURG

4

5

6

AV. D'AUDERGHEM

2

1

1/10.000ᵉ

© Brussels UrbiS, C.I.R.B.

1 cm = 100 m

500 m

A Portrait of

BRUSSELS

BRUXELLES
BRUSSEL
BRÜSSEL

Photos – Foto's – Photographs – Aufnahmen

Vincent Merckx

Textes – Teksten – Text – Texte

Georges-Henri Dumont
de l'Académie royale de Langue et de Littérature françaises

A Portrait of

BRUSSELS
BRUXELLES
BRUSSEL
BRÜSSEL

VINCENT MERCKX
EDITIONS

D epuis l'an 977, Charles de France, duc de Basse-Lotharingie, détient le comté de Bruocsella que lui a confié l'empereur Otton II. Le site, défendu par les marécages de la Senne, plaît à ce Carolingien; il bâtit un château sur l'île Saint-Géry dont il fait sa résidence habituelle entre deux expéditions militaires.

Dressé là où s'élève l'église des Riches Claires, ce *castrum* évoque encore les camps retranchés des Celtes et des Germains. La nuit, peu de monde dans l'île mais, le jour, elle est fort animée : voici les paysans amenant les récoltes des domaines ducaux, pour les entreposer dans les magasins; et puis, franchissant l'un des trois ponts de la Senne, voici les receveurs, les maires venant rendre leurs comptes aux notaires; et l'on rencontre aussi maints plaideurs qui, avant de se présenter aux échevins, discutent entre eux leurs causes. Quand le soleil décline, chacun quitte l'île, s'en retournant, qui vers son hameau planté au bord d'un affluent de la Senne, qui vers sa maison de torchis, là-bas au flanc d'un coteau.

Moins de cent ans plus tard, Bruxelles a pris l'allure d'une place commerciale, d'un *portus*. Là où la Senne cesse d'être navigable, on voit désormais les marchands se grouper autour d'un débarcadère.

Le comte Lambert II, dit Balderic, s'efforce d'accélérer cette évolution. Il confie à l'église Saint-Michel-au-Mont la châsse de sainte Gudule, jusqu'alors conservée dans la chapelle du *castrum*. Gudule apparaît déjà comme la sainte la plus populaire en ville, voire du Brabant. Sur la colline sablonneuse, la splendide église gothique lui consacra plus tard l'une de ses tours, dédiant l'autre à saint Michel, premier patron de la ville.

D'année en année, la cité prend plus d'importance. Au XIIᵉ siècle, le centre de la vie urbaine devient le marché installé sur un marais asséché, l'actuelle Grand-Place. Le prince a quitté son *castrum* de l'île Saint-Géry pour résider dans une forteresse édifiée sur le Coudenberg.

Entre-temps, la dynastie de Louvain cherche à unifier le Brabant et à contrôler la région d'entre Meuse et Rhin, plus précisément la route joignant le bassin rhénan au comté de Flandre en pleine prospérité. Cet objectif est atteint en 1288 par Jean Iᵉʳ de Brabant, sa victoire à Worringen est décisive pour l'avenir de Bruxelles.

Sous le règne de Jean Iᵉʳ, la ville voit s'achever sa première enceinte de pierre, au périmètre de quatre kilomètres. Cette puissante défense prend la forme d'un cœur... Derrière les remparts, la vie urbaine s'ordonne autour de quatre quartiers : le marché, le port, l'église des Saints-Michel-et-Gudule et le château ducal. Les bourgeois s'enrichissent, conquièrent des droits importants et forment une véritable aristocratie marchande qui détient tous les pouvoirs politiques de la ville.

Mais voici qu'à leur tour les gens des métiers veulent accéder au pouvoir : si l'industrie drapière connaît une telle prospérité, si son renom s'étend à l'Europe, n'en sont-ils pas les premiers artisans? Pour Bruxelles comme pour la plupart des villes belges, le XIVᵉ siècle se caractérise par une violente agitation sociale. Nobles, patriciens et plébéiens cherchent à se ravir mutuellement la prépondérance des affaires publiques. Privilèges et chartes, émeutes et châtiments se succèdent, entraînant l'appauvrissement du peuple. Calamité supplémentaire : en 1356, une guerre de succession éclate entre la duchesse Jeanne de Brabant et le comte de Flandre Louis de Male. Le mercredi 17 mars, les Flandriens plantent leur bannière sur une maison de la Grand-Place; ils sont maîtres de la ville. Pas pour longtemps! Dans la nuit pluvieuse du 24 octobre, le gentilhomme brabançon Everard 't Serclaes et une centaine d'hommes décidés escaladent le rempart, se ruent vers la Grand-Place, arrachent l'étendard du comte de Flandre flottant sur la maison l'Étoile. Cet exploit exalte les Bruxellois : armés de leurs instruments de travail, les bouchers, les rôtisseurs, les marmitons courent sus à l'occupant, éliminant bientôt la faible garnison flandrienne. La paix d'Ath met fin au conflit et, tirant la leçon des événements, les Bruxellois achèvent en 1383 un nouveau mur défensif comportant septante-quatre tours semi-circulaires et sept portes fortifiées.

Sous l'impulsion de la Maison de Bourgogne, les provinces belges s'unissent toujours davantage. En 1430, le Brabant est intégré à l'ensemble des Pays-Bas. Plus que les Gantois et les Brugeois, les Bruxellois soutiennent la politique centralisatrice de Philippe le Bon, car ils pressentent déjà le rôle qu'ils pourraient jouer au cœur d'une monarchie forte. Le Grand Duc d'Occident leur en sait gré : en 1459, c'est à Bruxelles qu'il installe sa Chambre des Comptes – Bruxelles qui commence à faire figure de capitale de l'Etat bourguignon.

À cette époque, la cour ducale du Coudenberg est fastueuse. La noblesse rivalise de luxe avec le prince. Les demeures des Clèves, Croy, Aerschot, Auxy ou de Fiennes étonnent l'étranger par l'abondance de leurs trésors d'art, la richesse de leur décoration. Tournois, fêtes, banquets, ommegangs, chapitres de l'ordre nouvellement créé de la Toison d'Or se succèdent dans Bruxelles qui reflète la gloire des Grands Ducs d'Occident.

Le Tournaisien Roger de le Pasture est le peintre officiel de la ville et a pris le nom de van der Weyden. Le Gantois Hugo van der Goes achève ses jours au Rouge-Cloître. C'est le temps des compositeurs Dufay, Ockegem, le Binchois; le temps où les arbalétriers édifient Notre-Dame du Sablon et où Jean van Ruysbroeck jette dans le ciel ce cri de joie triomphante qu'est la tour de l'hôtel de ville.

Les insurrections qui suivent la mort tragique de Charles le Téméraire en 1477, puis celle de sa fille Marie de Bourgogne en 1482, ne sont que des parenthèses, les derniers sursauts du particularisme local. Par une sage politique de modération, Philippe le Beau rétablit l'ordre et la prospérité.

Et voici que Charles Quint lance le pays dans la grande aventure européenne! Réceptions et visites princières fournissent au peuple de Bruxelles le prétexte à des fêtes hautes en couleurs, des cortèges à gaudrioles et des ripailles plantureuses. Mais à l'éclatante joie de

---

◁◁

*Le **parc du Cinquantenaire** fut créé en vue de l'Exposition Universelle de 1880 afin de célébrer les cinquante ans d'indépendance de la Belgique. Son aménagement est conforme au souhait du roi Léopold II, qui voulait que l'ancien plateau de Linthout devienne un lieu de promenade et de culture. Après l'achèvement en 1922 de l'aile donnant sur l'avenue des Nerviens, le Palais du Cinquantenaire reçut l'appellation définitive de Musées royaux d'Art et d'Histoire (à l'arrière-plan). Ceux-ci, parmi les plus riches d'Europe, exposent des œuvres majeures des quatre continents. La majestueuse rotonde de l'aile droite est coiffée d'une coupole néoclassique. La tourelle néo-gothique fut édifiée dans le parc par l'architecte Henri Beyaert, afin de promouvoir la pierre de Tournai lors de l'Exposition Universelle.*

*Het **Jubelpark** werd aangelegd met het oog op de Wereldtentoonstelling van 1880 en voor de viering van de vijftigjarige onafhankelijkheid van België. Het park is ontworpen volgens de wens van koning Leopold II, die wilde dat het voormalige Linthoutplateau een wandel- en cultuurfunktie kreeg. Na de voltooiing, in 1922, van de vleugel die uitgeeft op de Nerviërslaan, kreeg het Jubelpaleis zijn definitieve doel in de Koninklijke Musea voor Kunst en Geschiedenis (op de achtergrond). Deze musea, die tot de rijkste van Europa behoren, stellen belangrijke werken tentoon afkomstig uit de hele wereld. De majestueuze rotonde op de rechtervleugel draagt een neo-classicistische koepel. Het neo-gotische torentje werd door architect Henri Beyaert in het park opgetrokken om de Doornikse steen te promoten tijdens de Wereldtentoonstelling.*

*The **Cinquantenaire park** was created for the Universal Exhibition of 1880 celebrating fifty years of Belgian independence. It is laid out according to the wishes of Leopold II who wanted the Linthout plateau to become a promenade and cultural centre. After the wing facing the Avenue of the Nerviens was completed in 1922 the Cinquantenaire palace was designated the Royal Museums of Art and History (background). Major works from the four continents are displayed in these museums, among the richest in Europe. The majestic rotunda in the right wing is crowned with a neoclassical cupola. The Gothic Revival turret in the park was designed by the architect Henri Beyaert to promote Tournai stone during the Universal Exhibition.*

*Der **Jubelpark (parc du Cinquantenaire)** wurde anlässlich der Weltausstellung 1880 angelegt, um die fünfzigjährige Unabhängigkeit Belgiens zu feiern. Seine Gestaltung entspricht dem Wunsch König Leopolds II., der das ehemalige Plateau von Linthout zu einem Ort für Spaziergänge und Kultur machen wollte. Nach Vollendung des auf die Avenue des Nerviens weisenden Flügels im Jahre 1922 erhielt das Palais du Cinquantenaire seine endgültige Bezeichnung «Königliche Museen für Kunst und Geschichte» (im Hintergrund). Diese Museen, die zu den bestausgestatteten in Europa gehören, stellen Hauptwerke der vier Kontinente aus. Die majestätische Rotunde des rechten Flügels mit einer neoklassizistischen Kuppel bekrönt. Das neugotische Türmchen wurde von Architekt Henri Beyaert im Park errichtet, um den Stein von Tournai bei der Weltausstellung bekannt zu machen.*

vivre se mêlent déjà les méditations de l'esprit nouveau : à Anderlecht, à l'ombre de l'église Saints-Pierre-et-Guidon, l'humaniste Erasme définit la liberté des consciences; devant le Galgenberg où l'on exécute les condamnés, Vésale s'apprête à découvrir dans les cadavres des pendus les secrets du corps humain.

L'axe économique n'est plus la voie médiévale est-ouest; il va du sud au nord. Bruxelles n'y perd rien puisqu'elle se trouve, une nouvelle fois, sur son trajet et participe ainsi à la richesse du port d'Anvers. Le canal de Willebroek transforme, du reste, la ville en port maritime tandis qu'un service des postes à franc étrier est organisé par Jean-Baptiste de Tour et Tassis, en direction de l'Autriche et de l'Italie.

Hélas, à peine Charles Quint a-t-il abdiqué le 25 novembre 1555, devant les Etats généraux réunis au Coudenberg, que son fils, l'austère Philippe II, mène depuis Madrid une politique radicale. Il brime bientôt noblesse, clergé et cités. Il «espagnolise» le gouvernement, maintient dans le pays des troupes d'occupation, applique sans pitié les édits contre les opposants.

La colère fermente dans le peuple. Des seigneurs belges prennent la tête de la résistance et se liguent pour protester contre l'Inquisition. Traités de «gueux», ils font de cette injure un nom de ralliement. Les calvinistes se déchaînent, dévastant des centaines d'églises. Il fallait s'y attendre, la réaction de Philippe II est implacable : en 1567 arrive le duc d'Albe, chargé de noyer la rebellion dans le sang. Guillaume d'Orange, chef du mouvement de résistance, prend le large, mais les comtes d'Egmont et de Hornes sont arrêtés; ils ont la tête tranchée sur l'échafaud dressé sur la Grand-Place, en face de la Maison du Roi.

Cette inutile et odieuse provocation, voulue par Philippe II davantage que par le duc d'Albe, donne le signal de la révolution ouverte et déclarée.

En commençant par les provinces du Nord, le génial prince d'Orange tente d'affranchir tous les Pays-Bas de la dictature madrilène. Le 23 septembre 1577, il fait sa triomphale entrée à Bruxelles; les femmes s'agenouillent sur son passage. Mais le fanatisme a été allumé dans les cœurs : une minorité calviniste traque la majorité catholique des Bruxellois avec une rage digne des *tercios* espagnols. Les bourreaux se valent; seules la peste et la famine les surpassent en efficacité. Aussi bien, la population pousse-t-elle un soupir de soulagement lorsque, le 10 mars 1585, le duc de Parme Alexandre Farnèse reprend la ville pour le compte du roi d'Espagne.

La guerre politico-religieuse du XVIᵉ siècle se soldera par la rupture des anciennes dix-sept provinces de Charles Quint en deux blocs : au Nord, les Provinces Unies calvinistes; au Sud, les Pays-Bas catholiques.

Le règne des archiducs Albert et Isabelle (1598-1621) marque une pause heureuse dans les tourments de Bruxelles et du pays. Accalmie bienvenue de quelques décennies. Le temps d'élever de nombreuses églises en style baroque, le temps de mériter le titre d'auberge des princes en exil et déjà les troupes françaises de Louis XIV sont en vue. Le maréchal de Villeroi et ses septante mille hommes ont reçu l'ordre de prendre Bruxelles coûte que coûte. Le 13 août 1695, dix-huit pièces de gros calibres et vingt-cinq mortiers ouvrent le tir depuis les hauteurs de Scheut. Le bombardement durera trente-six heures. Trois mille bombes et douze cents boulets rouges s'abattent sur la cité de l'Archange, dont le centre se transforme bientôt en une mer de flammes. La tour de l'hôtel de ville est le point de mire, mais elle échappe au désastre. Cependant, l'hôtel de ville brûle avec ses tapisseries, ses trésors, ses tableaux fameux. Tout le quartier de la Grand-Place n'est plus que ruines fumantes. Seize églises, chapelles et couvents sont anéantis; trois mille huit cent cinquante maisons détruites : la ville résiste toujours. Aux remparts, les Bruxellois manquant de boulets tirent avec des pavés! Or, les Français ayant capitulé devant Namur, Villeroi abandonne précipitamment le siège de Bruxelles le 5 septembre.

Cinq années suffiront au magistrat de la ville, aux corporations et à quelques particuliers pour ressusciter la Grand-Place et en faire l'une des plus belles du monde.

Du XVIIIᵉ siècle et du régime autrichien amorcé en 1715, les Bruxellois retiendront surtout la bonhomie du gouverneur général Charles de Lorraine, épris de musique et de théâtre. Urbaniste avant la lettre, il dessine la future Place Royale à l'emplacement du palais du Coudenberg détruit dans l'incendie de 1731.

En 1789, Bruxelles participe à la révolution brabançonne ou plus exactement à la contre-révolution brabançonne contre l'empereur Joseph II, imbu des «Lumières» et soucieux de moderniser – sans y préparer les esprits – les institutions des Pays-Bas. Les États Belgiques Unis indépendants sont proclamés à Bruxelles le 11 janvier 1790, mais s'effondrent rapidement par décomposition inté-

rieure autant que par la victoire des troupes autrichiennes.

Durant le quart de siècle suivant, Bruxelles épouse les avatars militaires et diplomatiques de l'Europe occidentale : conquête par le général français Dumouriez en 1792; libération par les Autrichiens en 1793; réoccupation française en 1794; arrivée des Alliés européens en 1814; rattachement à la Hollande en 1815.

Guillaume Iᵉʳ d'Orange-Nassau, désigné par le Congrès de Vienne pour régner sur l'amalgame de la Belgique et de la Hollande, est homme d'affaires avisé, travailleur infatigable mais point homme d'État. Certes Bruxelles lui doit le renouveau de son commerce, son premier observatoire, son Jardin Botanique, son palais néo-classique du Prince d'Orange (actuellement le Palais des Académies), mais les Bruxellois, comme tous les Belges, se sentent des citoyens de seconde zone, ils ne jouissent ni de la liberté de presse ni de la liberté d'association.

En août 1830, excédés par les erreurs politiques de Guillaume Iᵉʳ au point d'oublier ses réels bienfaits matériels, les Belges chassent les Hollandais du pays. Le mouvement part de Bruxelles avec le grand air de la «Muette de Portici», chanté au théâtre de la Monnaie par le ténor à la mode La Feuillade. Et, contre toute attente, la révolution réussit son œuvre : une contre-offensive hollandaise échoue dans les combats du Parc de Bruxelles. Les provinces suivent l'exemple bruxellois : les hollandais sont chassés, la Belgique indépendante est née; Bruxelles en devient la capitale. Le Congrès National ne tarde pas à doter le pays d'une constitution démocratique qui réserve une place prééminente à la monarchie.

Léopold Iᵉʳ, le fondateur de la dynastie belge, est un diplomate-né mais il sait aussi susciter les initiatives économiques les plus intelligentes. Le 5 mai 1835, il préside l'inauguration du premier chemin de fer du continent. À la liaison ferroviaire Bruxelles-Malines s'en ajouteront promptement beaucoup d'autres, donnant à la Belgique une infrastructure de communications à laquelle elle devra une grande partie de sa prospérité au XIXᵉ siècle.

Léopold II, non content de doter son pays d'un empire africain, transforme profondément le visage urbanistique de Bruxelles. Il ne se lasse pas d'embellir la capitale : le voûtement de la Senne sous les boulevards du centre, la Bourse du Commerce, les Musées royaux des Beaux-Arts, le Palais Royal, le Palais de Justice, l'arcade du Cinquantenaire, les larges artères reliant Tervueren, Laeken, Boitsfort à la capitale, les parcs de Forest, Woluwe, Schaerbeek, Laeken... Selon les mots de Léon Daudet, il y a désormais deux Bruxelles : la ville avant et la ville après Léopold II.

À deux reprises, sous Albert Iᵉʳ d'abord, sous Léopold III ensuite, la Belgique se trouve entraînée dans une guerre mondiale, en dépit de sa neutralité. Bruxelles est chaque fois occupée par l'armée allemande. Entre les deux guerres, la reine Elisabeth, protectrice des arts, réussit à faire de la capitale belge l'incontestable point focal de la musique par la création du Concours international Eugène Ysaye. Et cette mission, Bruxelles continua de l'assumer avec éclat sous le règne du roi Baudouin.

Au temps où il était prince de Liège, le roi Albert II multiplia les témoignages de son intérêt pour le prestige de Bruxelles et, surtout, la sauvegarde de son patrimoine architectural. Sa présidence d'honneur de l'association «Quartier des Arts» n'était pas seulement un titre parmi d'autres; elle se révéla très active et souvent décisive dans le domaine de l'urbanisme.

Parce qu'elle fut longtemps une capitale aux allures provinciales dont les citoyens, loin de se monter du col, pêchent plutôt par modestie excessive, Bruxelles s'est toujours caractérisée par la tolérance et l'ouverture au monde. Depuis qu'elle est le siège principal des institutions de l'Union Européenne, «les douze mille fonctionnaires internationaux qui l'habitent, écrit Jacques De Decker, l'aiment pour sa manière inclassable, imprévue, insolite d'être banale et extraordinaire, quotidienne et universelle, d'avoir un rôle à jouer dans le destin de la planète tout en continuant de poursuivre son petit bonhomme de chemin de chef-lieu d'un État-tampon.»

L'OTAN s'étant, elle aussi, fixée dans son agglomération, Bruxelles est devenue la seule capitale au monde qui héberge trois corps diplomatiques : le premier auprès du gouvernement du Roi, le deuxième auprès de l'Union Européenne, le troisième auprès de l'OTAN.

Les grandes organisations internationales non gouvernementales ont suivi le mouvement; elles sont plus de cinq cents à avoir leur siège dans la capitale belge : un peu moins qu'à Paris mais davantage qu'à Londres, Genève et même New-York.

Bien sûr, le monde des affaires économiques et financières ne cesse d'être irrésistiblement attiré par ce qui est devenu le centre à la fois le plus ouvert, le plus disponible et le plus accueillant de l'Europe qui se fait.

Sedert 977 had Karel van Frankrijk, hertog van Neder-Lotharingen, het graafschap Bruocsella in leen, dat hem door keizer Otto II was afgestaan. Op die plaats, die op natuurlijke wijze beschermd werd door de moerassen van de Zenne, liet de Karolinger een burcht bouwen op het Sint-Gorikseiland. Daar vertoefde hij ook tussen twee krijgsondernemingen door.

Dit *castrum*, gelegen op de plaats waar thans de O.L.V.-der-Rijke-Klaren-kerk verrijst, leek nog op de Keltische en Germaanse legerkampen. 's Nachts zag het eilandje er nog tamelijk verlaten uit, maar overdag gonsde het er al van bedrijvigheid : boeren voerden er de oogst van het hertogelijk domein aan en sloegen ze op in de daarvoor bestemde bergplaatsen; ontvangers van taksen en schouten gingen één van de drie bruggen over de Zenne over en legden vervolgens rekenschap af in de schrijfkamer; klagers bepleitten er hun zaken alvorens door de wethouder te worden gehoord.

Als de zon onderging, verliet eenieder het eiland, de ene op weg naar zijn gehucht aan de één of andere bijrivier van de Zenne, de andere op weg naar zijn huisje met lemen muren ginder op de heuvelhelling.

Minder dan een eeuw later was Brussel al een portus waar druk handel werd gedreven. Waar de Zenne onbevaarbaar werd, was een aanlegsteiger aangelegd die de handelaars aantrok als een magneet.

De ook Balderik genoemde graaf Lambertus II bespoedigde deze ontwikkeling door het voordien in de kapel van het *castrum* bewaarde reliekschrijn van Sint-Goedele naar Sint-Michiel-op-den-Berg te laten overbrengen. Weldra was Sint-Goedele niet alleen de meest vereerde heilige van het stadje, maar van heel Brabant. Eén van de torens van de prachtige gotische kathedraal die later op de flank van de zandige heuvel zou verrijzen, draagt trouwens ook nu nog haar naam, terwijl de andere naar de aartsengel Michaël, de eerste beschermer van de stad, werd genoemd.

Jaar in jaar uit werd de stad belangrijker. In de 13de eeuw werd een drooggelegd moeras, de Nedermerct – de latere Grote Markt – het eigenlijke centrum van de handelsnederzetting, terwijl de hertog Sint-Goriks verliet en zijn intrek nam in zijn nieuwe vesting op Coudenberg.

Ondertussen hadden de hertogen van Leuven al pogingen gedaan om de eenwording van Brabant te bespoedigen. Ze wilden ook hun macht aan de hele streek tussen Maas en Rijn opdringen en zo de handelsroute tussen het Rijnland en het toen zeer welvarende Vlaanderen onder hun controle krijgen. Dankzij de overwinning die Jan I van Brabant in 1288 in Woeringen behaalde, slaagden ze erin dit doel te bereiken, hetgeen verstrekkende gevolgen had voor de verdere ontwikkeling van Brussel.

Onder diezelfde heerser werd de eerste, 4 km lange stadsmuur om Brussel gebouwd. Vanuit de lucht lijkt deze hartvormig te zijn. Achter deze omwalling draaide de handel en wandel van de Brusselaars als het ware om vier spillen : de markt, de haven, de St.-Michiels-en-St.-Goedelekerk en het hof van de hertog. De poorters werd rijker, dwongen belangrijke privileges af en vormden een handeldrijvend patriarchaat dat er volkomen in was geslaagd de kaarten van het politieke spel naar zijn hand te zetten.

Maar de gilden begonnen op hun beurt ook mee te dingen naar de macht : was de welvaart van de lakenindustrie en de bekendheid in heel Europa immers niet aan hen te danken? In Brussel, zoals in de meeste Belgische steden, was de 14de eeuw een periode van hevige sociale onlusten. Adel, patriciërs en ambachten trachtten het overwicht in het openbare leven te bemachtigen. Privileges en keuren, opstanden en onderdrukkingen volgden elkaar op en zaaiden armoede en ellende. Alsof dit nog niet volstond, barstte er in 1356 nog een successieoorlog los tussen de hertogin Johanna van Brabant en Lodewijk van Male, de geduchte graaf van Vlaanderen. Op woensdag 17 maart plantten de Vlamingen hun standaard op één der huizen van de Grote Markt : nu hadden zij het voor het zeggen in Brussel. Maar hun macht was van korte duur. Tijdens de onweerachtige nacht van 24 oktober bestormde de Brabantse edelman Everaerd 't Serclaes de vestingmuur met een honderdtal manschappen, haastte zich naar de Grote Markt en rukte de standaard van de graaf van Vlaanderen, die boven "De Sterre", wapperde, van het dak. Dit koene wapenfeit maakte de Brusselaars geestdriftig: beenhouwers, vleesbraders en koksjongens, elkeen gewapend met slagers- of keukengerei, vielen de bezetter aan en stelden het zwakke Vlaamse garnizoen in een mum van tijd buiten gevecht. Uiteindelijk werd het geschil door de vrede van Aat bijgelegd. De Brusselaars trokken een les uit de gebeurtenissen en voltooiden in 1383 de nieuwe stadsmuur met vierenzeventig halfcirkelvormige torens en zeven versterkte toegangspoorten.

Onder de hertogen van Bourgondië werden de banden tussen de Belgische provincies alsmaar hechter. In 1430 werd Brabant in het globale bestel van de Bourgondische Nederlanden geïntegreerd.

Meer dan de Gentenaars en de Bruggelingen steunden de Brusselaars de door Filips de Goede gevoerde centralisatiepolitiek, want ze hadden gauw door hoezeer een sterke monarchistische staatsvorm hun stad goed zou komen. De groothertog was hen daar dankbaar voor : in 1459 richtte hij er de Rekenkamer op. Vanaf dat ogenblik begon Brussel er echt uit te zien als de hoofdstad van het Bourgondische rijk.

In die periode wedijvert de adel in pracht en praal met de prinselijke praalzucht in Coudenberg. Buitenlandse bezoekers zijn met verstomming geslagen over de kunstschatten en de weelderige inrichtingen van de hoven van Kleef, Croy, Aerschot, Auxy en Fiennes. De tornooien, feesten, banketten, ommegangen, plechtige kapittelvergaderingen van de pas gestichte ridderorde van het Gulden Vlies volgden elkaar op in Brussel, wat de roem van de Westerse groothertogen nog deed stijgen.

De in Doornik geboren en getogen Roger de le Pasture werd toen onder de naam Rogier van der Weyden de officiële schilder van Brussel. De Gentenaar Hugo van der Goes kwam toen zijn leven in het Rode Klooster (in het Zoniënwoud) besluiten. Het was het tijdperk van de polyfonisten Dufay, Ockeghem, le Binchois. Het was eveneens in die tijd dat de kruisboogschutters met de bouw van de Onze-Lieve-Vrouw-van-de-Zavel Kerk begonnen en Jan van Ruysbroeck de toren van het stadhuis als een jubelkreet in de hemel liet oprijzen.

De opstanden die in 1477 op de tragische dood van Karel de Stoute en in 1482 op het overlijden van diens dochter Maria van Bourgondië volgden, waren maar kortstondige dwalingen, de laatste opflakkeringen van particularistische neigingen. De wijze, gematigde politiek van Filips de Schone stelde vlug weer orde op zaken en herstelde de welvaart.

Onmiddellijk daarna werd Brussel meegesleurd in het grote Europese avontuur van Karel de Vijfde. Vorstelijke ontvangsten en bezoeken boden de Brusselaars telkens weer de gelegenheid om kleurrijke feesten, mooie stoeten en Bruegeliaanse smulpartijen te houden. Maar door de triomf van het levensgenot heen schemerde de ernst van de nieuwe tijd: in de schaduw van de St.-Pieterskerk te Anderlecht bepaalde Erasmus de grenzen van het vrije geweten en aan de voet van de Galgenberg, waar de terdoodveroordeelden werden opgeknoopt, begon de ontleedkundige Vesalius de geheimen van het menselijk lichaam te peilen.

De grote handelsroute, die in de Middeleeuwen van het Westen (Brugge) naar het Oosten (Keulen) was gelopen, liep nu van noord naar zuid. Brussel boette er helemaal niets bij in dankzij zijn centrale ligging en leverde thans een niet te onderschatten bijdrage tot de rijkdom van de Antwerpse haven. Het kanaal van Willebroek maakte van Brussel zelfs een zeehaven, terwijl de koerierdienst die door Jan-Baptist van Thurn en Taxis op touw was gezet, voor een snelle verbinding met Oostenrijk en Italië zorgde.

Helaas! Pas had Keizer Karel op 25 november 1555 tijdens de plechtige vergadering van de Staten Generaal op de Coudenberg afstand gedaan van de troon, of zijn zoon, de strenge Filips II, begon onze gewesten vanuit Madrid hardhandig te regeren. Hij tergde adel en clerus, jaagde de steden tegen zich in het harnas, verspaanste regering en administratie, legerde bezettingstroepen in het land en paste de tegen de protestanten uitgevaardigde edicten meedogenloos toe.

Weldra waren alle gemoederen tegen hem verhit geraakt. Belgische edellieden voerden het verzet aan en spanden samen om protest aan te tekenen tegen de Inquisitie. Nadat ze voor geuzen waren uitgemaakt, maakten ze van "geuzen" hun wachtwoord. Opstandige calvinisten verwoestten honderden kerken. Zoals te verwachten, was de reactie van Filips II onverbiddelijk: in 1567 kreeg de hertog van Alva het bevel het verzet de kop in te drukken en het desnoods in bloed te smoren. Willem de Zwijger, de leider van het verzet, slaagde erin tijdig te ontsnappen, maar de graven van Egmont en van Hoorn werden opgepakt en op de Grote Markt vlak tegenover het Broodhuis onthoofd.

Deze nutteloze en afgrijselijke provocatie, die minder aan de hertog van Alva dan aan de onbuigzaamheid van Filips II valt toe te schrijven, was de lont in het kruitvat. Het smeulende oproer sloeg om in een onverholen opstand.

De geniale prins van Oranje vatte het plan op eerst de noordelijke provincies van de Spaanse Nederlanden van de Spaanse dictatuur te bevrijden. Op 23 september 1577 hield hij zijn triomfantelijke intrede in Brussel. Vrouwen knielden voor hem op zijn doortocht. Maar het fanatisme verblindde de geesten. Een calvinistische minderheid maakte jacht op de katholieke meerderheid van de Brusselaars, met een razernij die niet onderdeed voor die van de

Spanjaarden. De beulen waren eender en alleen pest en honger waren bloeddorstiger dan zij. Men begrijpt dan ook de zucht van opluchting die de bevolking slaakte, toen de hertog van Parma, Alexander Farnese, op 10 maart 1585 in opdracht van de koning van Spanje opnieuw bezit nam van de stad.

Deze 17de-eeuwse godsdienstoorlog, die tevens een politieke oorlog was, leidde tot de opsplitsing van de 17 Provinciën in twee blokken: de calvinistische Verenigde Provinciën in het noorden en de katholieke Spaanse Nederlanden in het zuiden.

De regering van de aartshertogen Albrecht en Isabella (1598-1621) bracht Brussel en het zwaar geteisterde land een welkome adempauze van enkele tientallen jaren. Deze twee decennia volstonden net om in Brussel talrijke barokke kerken uit de grond te doen verrijzen. Ze leverden de stad ook de bijnaam van toevluchtsoord voor verbannen vorsten op. Maar weldra stonden de Franse troepen van Lodewijk XIV voor de stadsmuren. Maarschalk de Villeroi en zijn 70.000 manschappen hadden het bevel gekregen Brussel kost wat kost in te nemen. Op 13 augustus 1695 begonnen hun 18 vuurmonden van groot kaliber en hun 25 mortiers de beschieting vanuit de hoogte van Scheut. Het bombardement duurde 36 uur. 3.000 bommen en 1.200 brandkogels werden afgevuurd op de door Sint-Michiel beschermde stad. Weldra was het centrum één grote vlammenzee. Al waren de vuurmonden allemaal op de torenspits van het stadhuis gericht, toch bleef precies die toren overeind. Ondertussen gingen in het stadhuis prachtige wandtapijten, beroemde schilderijen en andere kostbaarheden in vlammen op. Het duurde niet lang of de hele wijk rond de Grote Markt stond in brand. Maar de stad gaf zich niet over. Op de stadsmuren, waar de munitie schaars was geworden, werden dikke straatstenen als kogels gebruikt. Nadat Frankrijk voor Namen een zware nederlaag was toegebracht, brak Villeroi op 5 september inderhaast het beleg op.

Amper vijf jaar volstonden voor de magistraat, de gilden en enkele welstellende privépersonen om de Grote Markt weer op te laten bouwen en er één van de mooiste pleinen ter wereld van te maken.

Van de 18de eeuw en van het Oostenrijkse bewind (vanaf 1715) is bij de Brusselaars vooral de joviale figuur van de landvoogd Karel van Lorreinen, een groot muziek- en toneelliefhebber, blijven voortleven. Met voor die tijd uiterst moderne stedebouwkundige opvattingen tekende hij na de brand van het paleis op de Coudenberg in 1731 de plattegrond van het latere Koningsplein.

In 1789 nam Brussel deel aan de Brabantse revolutie – of beter tegenrevolutie – tegen keizer Jozef II, die de ideeën van de Verlichting in het daarvoor nog niet rijpe land ingang had willen doen vinden. Op 11 januari 1792 werden in Brussel de Verenigde Belgische Staten ten doop gehouden, maar interne verscheurdheid en vooral de militaire overwinning van de Oostenrijkers maakten weldra een einde aan het experiment.

Tijdens de daarop volgende kwarteeuw deelde Brussel in de wisselvalligheden van de toenmalige Europese politiek: de verovering door de Franse generaal Dumouriez in 1792; de bevrijding door de Oostenrijkers in 1793; de nieuwe bezetting door Frankrijk in 1794; het optreden en ingrijpen van de Bondgenoten in 1814; de aanhechting bij Nederland in 1815.

Willem I van Oranje-Nassau was door het Congres van Wenen aangewezen als heerser over het Koninkrijk der Nederlanden (de samensmelting van België en Holland). Hij was een bedachtzaam zakenman en noest werker, maar geen staatshoofd. De heropleving van de handelsactiviteit, het eerste observatorium, de Kruidtuin en het neoklassieke paleis van de Prins van Oranje heeft Brussel ongetwijfeld aan hem te danken. Maar, zoals alle Belgen, voelden ook de Brusselaars zich als tweederangsburgers behandeld, omdat ze van het recht op persvrijheid en op vrijheid van vereniging waren verstoken.

In augustus 1830 waren de Belgen zodanig over de politieke flaters van Willem I ontstemd dat ze er de feitelijk genoten materiële weldaden bij vergaten en de Hollanders het land uit joegen. De opstand brak in Brussel uit op de tonen van de grote aria uit "De Stomme van Portici" die in de Muntschouwburg door de door het publiek verafgode tenor La Feuillade werd gezongen. Tegen alle verwachting in slaagde de revolutie in haar opzet: het tegenoffensief van onze noorderburen liep dood in de Warande, het Park van Brussel. De Belgische provincies volgden dadelijk het door Brussel gestelde voorbeeld. Na de verdrijving van de Nederlanders was België eindelijk onafhankelijk en Brussel de hoofdstad van de nieuwe staat. Het Nationaal Congres begon meteen een democratische grondwet uit te werken en aan een staatsstructuur te sleutelen waarvan de erfelijke monarchie de eigenlijke sluitsteen is.

Leopold I, de stichter van het Belgische koningshuis, was een geboren diplomaat die tevens wel doordachte economische initiatieven wist te nemen of aan te moedigen. Op 5 mei 1835 huldigde hij de eerste spoorweg op het continent in. Aan de spoorwegverbinding Brussel-Mechelen werden gauw andere spoorlijnen toegevoegd, zodat België over het verkeersnet beschikte dat ten grondslag lag aan het welvaartspeil dat het in de 19de eeuw bereikte.

Leopold II was niet alleen de stichter van een koloniaal rijk in Afrika. Hij zorgde ook voor ingrijpende veranderingen in het stadsbeeld van Brussel. Zonder verpozen begunstigde hij al wat tot de verfraaiing van de hoofdstad bijdroeg: de overwelving van de Zenne onder de lanen in het centrum, de bouw van de Beurs, de Koninklijke Musea voor Schone Kunsten, het Koninklijk Paleis, het Justitiepaleis, de triomfboog in het Jubelpark, de lange verkeersaders die Tervuren, Laken en Bosvoorde met het centrum verbinden, de parken van Vorst, Woluwe, Schaarbeek en Laken enz.

Volgens het geestige gezegde van Léon Daudet bestonden er vanaf dat ogenblik twee steden die allebei Brussel heten: de stad die voor de troonsbestijging van Leopold II had bestaan, en de stad die hij als het ware uit de grond had gestampt.

Twee keer, eerst onder Albert I, daarna weer onder Leopold III, raakte België ondanks zijn neutraliteit in een wereldoorlog verwikkeld. Brussel werd telkens door de Duitsers bezet. Tussen die twee oorlogen slaagde koningin Elizabeth, de beschermster der kunsten, erin van de Belgische hoofdstad één van de voornaamste brandpunten van het internationale muziekleven te maken dankzij de internationale Eugène Ysaye-wedstrijd. Ook onder koning Boudewijn heeft Brussel zich met succes van deze taak gekweten.

Reeds als prins van Luik gaf koning Albert II blijk van zijn belangstelling voor de uitstraling van Brussel en vooral voor het behoud van zijn bouwkundig patrimonium. Erevoorzitter te zijn van de vereniging "Kunstwijk" was voor hem niet zomaar een eretitel : hij nam actief, vaak zelfs op doorslaggevende wijze deel aan de besluitvorming op stedebouwkundig vlak.

Brussel was eeuwenlang een hoofdstad met provinciale allures. Verre van het hoog in hun bol te hebben waren en zijn de Brusselaars eerder geneigd tot een haast overdreven aandoende bescheidenheid. Daarom werd Brussel altijd gekenmerkt door verdraagzaamheid en kosmopolitische openheid. Sinds het de hoofdzetel van de instellingen van de Europese Gemeenschap is geworden, wordt het, zoals Jacques De Decker terecht schrijft, "door de 12.000 internationale functionarissen die er vertoeven, bemind om de haast niet onder woorden te brengen, onvoorspelbare en ongewone wijze waarop het triviale en het buitengewone, het bijzondere en het algemene er samengaan en deze stad haar rol in de wereldpolitiek speelt, terwijl ze als hoofdstad van een bufferstaat gewoon haar gangetje blijft gaan."

Nu ook de NAVO zich in één der gemeenten van de Brusselse agglomeratie heeft gevestigd, is Brussel de enige hoofdstad ter wereld met een drievoudig corps diplomatique: één benoemd bij de regering van het koninkrijk, een ander bij de Europese Gemeenschap en weer een ander bij de NAVO.

De grote internationale niet-gouvernementele instellingen hebben dat voorbeeld gevolgd. Meer dan vijfhonderd hebben hun zetel of vertegenwoordigers in de Belgische hoofdstad, die in dit opzicht nog even voor Parijs onderdoet, maar Londen, Genève en zelfs New York al heeft voorbijgestreefd.

Het ligt trouwens voor de hand dat zakenwereld en haute-finance zich onweerstaanbaar door deze stad voelen aangetrokken, die het meest toegankelijke, ruimhartige en gastvrije middelpunt van ons Europa in wording is geworden.

In 977 Emperor Otto II gave the county of Bruocsella to Charles of France, Duke of Lower Lotharingia. The Carolingian built a stronghold on the island of St. Géry, a site protected by the marshes of the Senne river, which also became his principal residence between military campaigns.

The church of the Riches-Claires now stands on the site of this fort which resembled a Celto-Germanic entrenched camp or castrum. Although few people stayed on the island at night, during the day it was a hive of activity. Let us imagine peasants bringing harvests from the ducal estates to store in the warehouses, tax collectors and mayors coming to present their accounts to notaries, litigants discussing their cases together before appearing in court... At sunset they will leave the town for a little hamlet on a tributary of the Senne, or a wattle-and-daub house on a hillside.

In less than a hundred years Brussels had become a thriving commercial centre and one would have seen groups of merchants gathered at the landing stage where the Senne ceased to be navigable.

Count Lambert II, called Balderic, encouraged this development. He gave the reliquary of Saint Gudule, the most popular saint of the town, and indeed of all Brabant, previously kept in the chapel of the castrum, to the church of Saint Michael-on-the-Mount. Later, one of the towers of a magnificent Gothic church built on the sandy hill would be dedicated to her, the other being given to St. Michael, the first patron saint of the town.

◁◁

*Passionné d'automobile, Ghislain Mahy a rassemblé une prodigieuse collection de plus de 900 véhicules de tous types. Dans le grand hall de l'esplanade du Cinquantenaire, **Autoworld** raconte, par la présence de quelque 450 véhicules, l'histoire de l'automobile depuis la voiture à pétrole de 1886.*

Dès le début, les constructeurs belges se montrèrent inventifs et les marques belges furent à la pointe du progrès sur le plan technique comme sur celui du confort. Mais la crise économique de 1929 entraîna le déclin puis, après la seconde Guerre mondiale, la disparition de la création automobile belge. Son industrie se reconvertit alors dans le montage de voitures de marques étrangères.

*Het is de vurige bewonderaar van automodellen Ghislain Mahy gelukt een prachtige verzameling van meer dan 900 voertuigen van haast alle merken bijeen te brengen. In de grote hal van het Jubelpark begint **Autoworld** met de eerste benzinewagen van 1886 en vertelt ons de geschiedenis van de auto aan de hand van 450 modellen.*

De Belgische autoconstructeurs waren in het begin bijzonder creatief en van 1895 tot 1914 behoorden de Belgische merken qua technische snufjes en gerieflijkheid tot de allerbeste. De economische crisis van 1929 werd vooral voor luxe-auto's noodlottig. Ze leidde tot de verkwijning en, na de Tweede Wereldoorlog, tot de verdwijning van de Belgische auto-industrie, behalve dat er nog tal van buitenlandse merken worden geassembleerd.

*The automobile enthusiast Ghislain Mahy has assembled an enormous collection of over 900 vehicles of all types. **Autoworld**, at the Cinquantenaire, follows the history of the automobile from the gasoline-fired car of 1886 to modern days in an exhibition grouping 450 vehicles.*

From the beginning of the industry the Belgians were highly inventive and from 1895 to 1914 were in the forefront on the technical side as well as that of comfort. Decline set in with the financial crisis of 1929 and after World War II the Belgian automobile industry converted from building its own cars to assembling foreign-made ones.

*Dem leidenschaftlichen Sammler alter Automobile aller Marken Ghislain Mahy ist es gelungen, sich über 900 Fahrzeuge für seine Sammlung zu verschaffen. In der großen Halle des Cinquantenaire beginnt **Autoworld** mit dem ersten Auto mit Benzinmotor von 1886 und erzählt anhand von 450 Autos die ganze Geschichte des Automobils.*

Von Anfang an waren die belgischen Konstrukteure mit dabei, und von 1895 bis 1914 gehörten ihre Modelle zu den technisch besten und den am bequemsten ausgestatteten. Die Wirtschaftskrise von 1929 traf besonders Luxusmarken. Seitdem ging die belgische Autoindustrie zurück und verschwand nach dem Zweiten Weltkrieg ganz von der Bildfläche oder stellte sich auf die Montage ausländischer Marken um.

The town grew in importance yearly; in the 13th century the focus of urban life was the market, held on a drained swamp called the Nedermerct, now the Grand-Place. The prince moved his residence from the castrum on the island to a fortress on Coudenberg.

At this time the House of Louvain was striving to unify Brabant and thus control the region between the Meuse and the Rhine, and especially the route linking the Rhine basin to the prosperous County of Flanders. This objective was achieved in 1288 by the victory of John I of Brabant at Worringen which was very important for the future of Brussels.

Under John I the town received its first stone walls, nearly four kilometers in perimeter, enclosing a heartshaped area. Behind the ramparts urban life centered on four areas : the market, the port, the church of Saints Michael and Gudule, and the ducal castle. Prosperous citizens acquired important rights and formed a merchant aristocracy which controlled the town politically.

However, the craftsmen also wanted a share of this power, arguing that the prosperity of the cloth trade and its renown throughout Europe was based on their labour. Like most Belgian cities, Brussels suffered from violent social unrest during the 14th century. Nobles, patricians and plebeians fought amongst themselves for political dominance, and privileges and charters, riots and punishment followed in a weary round, leading to the impoverishment of the people.

In 1356 another disaster struck when a war of succession broke out between Jeanne, Duchess of Brabant, and Louis de Male, Count of Flanders. On Wednesday, March 17th supporters of the House of Flanders raised their banner on a house on the Grand-Place. Flanders had taken the town – but not for long!

On the rainy night of October 24th Everard 't Serclaes, a gentleman from Brabant and a hundred determined men, scaled the walls, sped to the Grand-Place and tore down the standard of the Count of Flanders which floated above the house of the Star. This exploit heartened the people of Brussels and butchers, bakers and candlestick makers armed with the tools of their trade threw themselves on the occupiers, soon defeating the weak garrison. The conflict was ended by the Peace of Ath and, having learned its lesson, Brussels built a new defensive wall with seventy-four semi-circular towers and seven fortified gates, completed in 1383.

The Belgian provinces, under the influence of the House of Burgundy, became more united and in 1430 Brabant was integrated into the Low Countries. Brussels, aware of the advantage of being at the heart of a strong monarchy, supported the centralizing policies of Philip the Good more than Ghent or Bruges. The Grand Duke of the West was grateful, and in 1459 established his revenue courts in Brussels which was assuming the role of capital of the Burgundian state.

At this time the ducal court of Coudenberg was sumptuous and the nobility rivaled the Prince in luxury. The many works of art in the richly decorated residences of the Cleves, Croy, Aerschot and de Fiennes families impressed visiting strangers. Tournaments, festivals, banquets, ommegangs and meetings of the newly founded Order of the Golden Fleece were common in Brussels, reflecting the glory of the Grand Dukes of the West.

Roger de le Pasture from Tournai became the official city painter and changed his name to van der Weyden. Hugo van der Goes from Ghent lived out his days at Rouge-Cloître. Composers such as Dufay, Ockeghem and le Binchois provided music. The crossbowmen built Our Lady of the Sablon, and the beautiful spire of the Town Hall was raised by Jan van Ruysbroeck.

The uprisings after the tragic death of Charles the Bold in 1477 and again following the death of his daughter Mary in 1482, were the last gasp of local particularism. Philip the Fair re-established order and prosperity by his wise and moderate policies.

Under Charles V the country became involved in the great game of European politics. Receptions and princely visits provided the people of Brussels with excuses for colorful festivals, amusing parades and gluttonous feasts. However, another spirit coexisted alongside this hearty and worldly activity and in Anderlecht, in the shadow of St. Peter's church the humanist, Erasmus was defining liberty of conscience, while Vesalius sought the secrets of the human body by dissecting the corpses stolen from Gallow's Hill.

The economy was no longer oriented on the old mediæval East-West axis, but now ran North-South. This did not affect Brussels which was on this route as well, and the city also shared in the prosperity of the port of Antwerp. The Willebroek canal made the city a maritime port as well, while a mounted postal service to Austria and Italy was founded by Jean-Baptiste of Tour and Tassis.

After the abdication of Charles V before the States-General at

Coudenberg in 1555, things took a turn for the worse. From Madrid Charles' son, the grim Philip II proclaimed new, radical policies, bullying the nobility, clergy and cities. Government posts were filled by Spaniards, Spanish troops were garrisoned in the country and edicts against Protestants were mercilessly enforced.

The people became angry and the Belgian nobles leading the opposition to Philip's policies allied themselves in protest against the Inquisition. Dismissed scornfully as *gueux*, or beggars, they adopted this insult as their rallying cry. The Calvinists revolted and sacked hundreds of churches. The reaction of Philip II was to be expected and in 1567 he unleashed the "Spanish Fury" under the Duke of Alba to crush the revolt in blood. William of Orange, leader of the rebels, escaped but the Counts of Egmont and Hoorn were arrested and decapitated on a scaffold erected in front of the King's House on the Grand-Place. This foolish and hateful action, more the wish of Philip II than of Alba himself, sparked an open declaration of rebellion.

The much-loved Prince of Orange strove to liberate all the Low Countries from the dictatorship of Madrid, beginning with the Northern provinces. On September 23, 1577 he entered Brussels in triumph, women kneeling as he passed. However, fanaticism had been unleashed and a small Calvinist minority began to hound the Catholic majority of Brussels as implacably as they themselves had been by the Spanish. Executioners worked overtime and plague and famine claimed their share of victims as well. When Alexander Farnese, Duke of Parma recaptured the city for the King of Spain on March 10, 1585 the population greeted him with relief.

The political and religious war of the 16th century ended with the division of the old seventeen provinces of Charles V into two blocs : The Calvinist United Provinces in the north and the Catholic Low Countries in the south.

A few tranquil decades under the reign of the Archidukes Albert and Isabelle (1598-1621) were a welcome respite in the turbulent history of Brussels and the country. There was just enough time to build a few baroque churches and to gain a reputation as a refuge for princes in exile before the troops of Louis XIV hove into sight.

Marshal Villeroi and his 70,000 men were commanded to take Brussels, whatever the cost. On August 13, 1685 eighteen large bombards and twenty-five mortars opened fire from the heights of Scheut. The shelling lasted 36 hours and three thousand shells and twelve hundred red-hot cannonballs rained upon the city of the Archangel. The centre was a sea of flames but the spire of the Town Hall, the main target, escaped destruction. The Town Hall itself, its tapestries, treasure and works of art, was burned out.

The neighbourhood around the Grand-Place was reduced to smoking ruins. Sixteen churches, chapels and convents were totally destroyed, as well as 3850 houses, but still the city resisted. From the walls the people of Brussels fired cobblestones, for want of ammunition. Meanwhile, the French army at Namur had surrendered and on September 5th Villeroi suddenly ended the siege of Brussels.

Within five years the city magistrate, with the aid of the guilds and a few private citizens had completely rebuilt the Grand-Place, making it one of the most beautiful in the world.

In 1715 the Austrians took over the country and from this regime Brussels has fond memories of the jovial Governor-General, Charles of Lorraine, patron of music and theater. Charles was an enthusiastic town-planner and designed the present Place Royale to replace the old Coudenberg palace which burned down in the fire of 1731.

In 1789 Brussels participated in the Brabant revolution, or to be accurate, counter-revolution against Joseph II. The Austrian Emperor was a disciple of the Enlightenment and wished to modernize the institutions of the Low Countries but had not prepared the minds of the people. An independent United States of Belgium was proclaimed in Brussels on January 11, 1790 but collapsed rapidly, as much from internal dissension as from Austrian military might.

During the following quarter century Brussels endured the same diplomatic and military turmoil as the rest of Europe. Conquered by the French General Dumouriez in 1792, it was liberated by the Austrians in 1793 and then retaken by the French in 1794. The allies against Napoleon took it in 1814 and in 1815 it was given to the Dutch.

William I of Orange-Nassau, designated as ruler of a united Holland and Belgium by the Congress of Vienna, was an astute businessman and an energetic worker, but not at all a statesman. Brussels owes him its renewed commerce, the Observatory, the Botanical Gardens, the neo-classical palace of the Prince of Orange,

now the Academy, but the people of Brussels, like all the Belgians, felt like second-class citizens, having neither the right to a free press nor freedom of association.

In August 1830 the Belgians, so exasperated by William's political blunders that they forgot the real material benefits of his reign, drove the Dutch from the country. The rising began at the Monnaie opera house in Brussels when the popular tenor La Feuillade sang the great aria from "La Muette de Portici". Against all expectations the revolt archieved its objective and a Dutch counteroffensive failed at the battle of the park of Brussels. The provinces followed the example of the city, expelling the Dutch, and an independent Belgium, with Brussels as its capital, was born. A National Assembly quickly drew up a democratic constitution with an hereditary monarchy as its keystone.

Leopold I, founder of the Belgian Royal House, was a born diplomat who also encouraged intelligent economic policies. He inaugurated the first railway on the Continent, running from Brussels to Mechelen, on May 5, 1835. More lines were built quickly, giving Belgium a communications infrastructure which contributed greatly to the prosperity of the 19th century.

Leopold II not only gave his country an African empire but changed the appearance of Brussels profoundly. He worked unflaggingly to beautify his capital and was responsible for the downtown boulevards covering the Senne as well as the Stock Exchange, the Royal Fine Arts Museums, the Royal Palace, the Law Courts and the Cinquantenaire. He also devised the majestic boulevards linking Tervuren, Laeken and Boitsfort to the capital as well as the parks of Forest, Woluwe, Schaerbeek, Laeken and much more. Leon Daudet remarked that henceforth there were two Brussels : before Leopold II and after Leopold II.

Despite its declared neutrality, Belgium has been dragged twice into world wars, once under Albert I and again under Leopold III. Both times Brussels was occupied by the German army. Between the wars Queen Elizabeth, wife of Albert I and a great patron of arts, made the Belgian capital a renowned centre of music by founding the Eugene Isaye International Competition. Under King Baudouin, Brussels continued this tradition brilliantly.

King Albert II, when he was Prince of Liège, often gave evidence of his concern for the prestige of Brussels and particularly for the defense of its architectural heritage. His position as Honorary Chairman of the "Arts Quarter Association" was not merely honorific but active, and often decisive in the field of town planning.

The citizens of Brussels, for so long the capital of a small state, tend to err perhaps on the side of modesty and are characterized by a tolerant and open attitude to the world. The city is now the principal seat of the bodies of the European Community and, writes Jacques De Decker "is appreciated by the twelve thousand international civil servants who live there because it is difficult to categorize, full of surprises, an unusual mix of the ordinary and the extraordinary, the particular and the universal, playing a part in the destiny of the world while continuing its modest role as the capital of a buffer state."

Since NATO has also established its headquarters in greater Brussels the city is the only one in the world to host three diplomatic corps : the first is accredited to the Kingdom, the second to the European Community and the third to NATO.

More than 500 non-governmental international bodies have head offices in Brussels, a few less than Paris but more than London, Geneva and even New York. And, of course, the financial and business world is drawn irresistibly to what has become the most open, hospitable and receptive centre in the new Europe.

Im Jahre 977 belehnte Kaiser Otto II. Karl von Frankreich, den Herzog Niederlothringens, mit der Grafschaft Bruocsella. Die durch die Senne und ihre sumpfigen Ufer geschützte Stellung gefiel dem Karolinger. Er baute eine Festung auf der Insel Saint-Géry und, wenn es seine Feldzüge zuließen, nahm er dort seinen Wohnsitz.

Diese Festung – sie befand sich ungefähr da, wo heute die Kirche der Riches-Claires (reichen Klarissen) steht – glich noch den durch Schanzarbeiten befestigten Lagern der Kelten und Germanen. Die nachts wie verlassen daliegende Insel war tagsüber von regem Leben erfüllt: Bauern fuhren den Ertrag der herrschaftlichen Ländereien in die Lagerräume; auf den drei Brücken, die sich über der Senne wölbten, kamen Verwalter von Meiereien daher, um höherenorts Bericht zu erstatten; Prozessführer trafen sich und vereinbarten dieses und jenes, bevor sie vor dem Schöffen vorstellig wurden.

Bei Sonnenuntergang verließen die Besucher die Insel und begaben sich in ihren Weiler an einem der Nebenflüsse der Senne oder in ihr Haus aus Stroh- oder Kleiberlehm am Hügelabhang.

Kaum ein Jahrhundert später hatte Brüssel bereits das Aussehen eines "portus", eines Handelshafens. Da, wo die Senne aufhörte, schiffbar zu sein, hatten Kaufleute um die Anlegestelle herum eine Siedlung geschaffen.

Graf Lambert II., auch Balderic genannt, beschleunigte diese Entwicklung. Den bislang in der Kapelle der Festung aufbewahrten Schrein der heiligen Gudula ließ er in die Sankt-Michaelskirche am Berg überführen, so dass die Heilige bald nicht nur in der Stadt, sondern auch in ganz Brabant verehrt wurde. Jahrhunderte später sollte sich auf dem sandigen Hügel eine gotische Kathedrale erheben, deren beide Türme noch heute den Namen bzw. den ersten Schutzpatrons der Stadt, des Erzengels Michael, tragen.

Von Jahr zu Jahr nahm die Bedeutung der Stadt zu. Im 13. Jh. spielte sich das Stadtleben bereits hauptsächlich auf einem durch Trockenlegung entstandenen Platz ab, den man "Nedermerct" (unteren Markt) nannte, und der sich allmählich zum heutigen Marktplatz (Grand-Place) entwickelte. Inzwischen war der Herzog aus seiner Festung auf der Insel Saint-Géry in sein Schloss auf dem Coudenberg umgezogen.

Damals versuchte das Herrscherhaus von Löwen, Brabant zusammenzuschließen und das Gebiet zwischen Maas und Rhein, genauer gesagt die Handelstraße, die das Rheinland mit der reichen Grafschaft Flandern verband, unter seine Kontrolle zu bringen. Es erreichte dieses Ziel 1288, als Johann I. von Brabant bei Worringen siegte. Dieser Sieg war für die Zukunft Brüssels von entscheidender Bedeutung.

Unter Johann I. wurden auch die ersten, 4 km langen Stadtmauern um Brüssel gebaut. Hinter diesem Verteidigungsgürtel, dessen Verlauf in etwa dem Umriss eines Herzens glich, befanden sich die vier Stadtteile und ihr jeweiliger Mittelpunkt: der Marktplatz, der Hafen, die dem Erzengel Michael und der heiligen Gudula geweihte Kirche und das herzogliche Schloss. Die Bürger gelangten zu Wohlstand, erwarben wichtige Privilegien und bildeten faktisch eine kaufmännische Aristokratie, welche die politische Macht völlig an sich gerissen hatte.

Doch nun erschienen die Zünfte auf dem Plan und machten ihre Machtansprüche geltend. Waren sie nicht die Urheber des materiellen Wohlstands, den die in ganz Europa berühmten Tuchwebereien um sich verbreitet hatten? Wie die meisten belgischen Städte wurde auch Brüssel im 14. Jh. von sozialen Unruhen heimgesucht. Adel, Patrizier und Zünfte versuchten, sich gegenseitig aus dem Sattel zu heben. Privilegien und Freibriefe, Aufstände und Strafaktionen folgten aufeinander und machten die Armen noch ärmer. Als ob dies nicht genügte, brach 1356 ein Erbfolgekrieg zwischen der Herzogin Johanna I. von Brabant und dem Grafen von Flandern Ludwig van Male aus. Am Mittwoch, dem 17. März, pflanzten die Flamen ihre Standarte auf eines der Häuser am Marktplatz. Doch ihre Herrschaft währte nicht lange. In der regnerischen Nacht des 24. Oktobers erkletterte ein Edelmann aus Brabant, Everaert 't Serclaes, mit einer Hundertschaft die Stadtmauern, stürmte zum Marktplatz und riss die Standarte des Grafen von Flandern vom Dach des "Etoile" (Stern) genannten Hauses herunter. Die wagemutige Tat entflammte die Herzen der Einwohner. Mit Fleischerbeilen und Küchengerät in ihren Händen bestürmten Metzger, Köche und Küchenjungen die zahlenmäßig unterlegene flämische Besatzung und vertrieben sie. Schließlich setzte der Frieden von Ath den Streitigkeiten ein Ende. Die durch Schaden klug gewordenen Brüsseler errichteten 1381 neue Stadtmauern. Diese umfassten 74 halbrunde Türme und 7 befestigte Stadttore.

Die auf Zentralisation gerichtete Politik des Hauses von Burgund hatte einen immer enger werdenden Zusammenschluss der belgischen Provinzen zur Folge. 1430 wurde Brabant den burgundischen Niederlanden einverleibt. Mehr als Brügge und Gent war Brüssel jedoch der Zentralismus Philipps des Guten willkommen, denn es ahnte voraus, dass ihm in einer starken monarchischen Staatsform die Führungsrolle zufallen würde. Der Großfürst des Abendlandes wusste ihm Dank: 1459 errichtete er den Rechnungshof in Brüssel, das dadurch die Hauptstadt des burgundischen Reiches zu sein schien.

In dieser Zeit gehörte der Hof des Herzogs auf dem Coudenberg zu den prunkvollsten. In den Herrenhäusern derer von Kleef, Croy, Aerschot, Auxy oder Fiennes versetzten der Reichtum an Kunstgegenständen und die Pracht der Ausgestaltung die Besucher in Erstaunen. Turniere, Feste, große Bankette, Umzüge, Generalkapitel des vor kurzem ins Leben gerufenen Ordens des Goldenen Vlieses folgten einander und spiegelten den Ruhm der Großherzöge von Burgund wider.

Der aus Tournai stammende Roger de le Pasture wurde unter dem Namen Van der Weyden offizieller Maler der Stadt. Der aus Gent gebürtige Hugo van der Goes beschloss sein Leben in der Priorei des Rouge-Cloître. Es war auch das Zeitalter der Meister der polyphonen Musik Dufay, Ockegem, le Binchois. Fast zur gleichen Zeit bauten die Armbrustschützen die Kirche Notre-Dame du Sablon, und Jan van Ruysbroeck ließ den Rathausturm wie einen Triumphschrei gen Himmel steigen.

Die Aufstände nach dem tragischen Tod Karls des Kühnen 1477 sowie die Unruhen nach dem Hinscheiden seiner Tochter Maria von Burgund 1482 waren nur beiläufige Ereignisse, ein letztes Aufflackern partikularistischer Bestrebungen. Alsbald stellte die weise, besonnene Politik Philipps des Schönen Ordnung und Wohlstand wieder her.

Dann folgte die Zeit, in der Kaiser Karl V. das Land in das große Abenteuer seiner europäischen Politik einbezog. Empfänge und Fürstenbesuche boten dem Volk Gelegenheit zu bunten Festen, Umzügen mit Ulk und Mummenschanz und breugelhaften Schlemmereien. Doch in die triumphierende Lebensfreude mischte sich bereits das tiefschürfende Denken des neuen Geistes: In Anderlecht, im Schatten der St.-Peterskirche, bestimmte der Humanist Erasmus die Grenzen der Gewissensfreiheit, und am Fuße des Galgenbergs, auf dem die Verurteilten gehängt wurden, ging Vesallus daran, in den Leichen der Erhängten den Geheimnissen des menschlichen Körpers nachzuspüren.

Die Achse des wirtschaftlichen Lebens verlief nicht mehr wie im Mittelalter von Osten nach Westen, sondern von Süden nach Norden. Brüssel litt nicht im geringsten darunter, denn wieder befand es sich auf dem Weg und durfte am Reichtum der aufblühenden Hafenstadt Antwerpen teilhaben. Der Kanal von Willebroek machte es sogar möglich, in Brüssel einen Seehafen zu bauen, indes Johann Baptist von Thurn und Taxis einen Postdienst im gestreckten Galopp nach Italien und Österreich ins Leben rief.

Doch kaum hatte Karl V. am 25. November 1555 vor den feierlich auf Schloss Coudenberg versammelten Generalstaaten dem Thron entsagt, so begann auch schon sein Sohn, der gestrenge Philipp II., von Madrid aus seine verhängnisvolle Politik durchzusetzen. Er schikanierte Adel, Klerus und Städte, hispanisierte die Behörden, zwang dem Volk Besatzungstruppen auf und bestand auf der rücksichtslosen Vollstreckung seiner Erlasse gegen die Protestanten.

Es schwelte Unruhe im Volke. Belgische Edelleute stellten sich an die Spitze des Widerstands und verbündeten sich in ihrem Protest gegen die Inquisition. Für die als "Geusen" Verspotteten wurde dieses Schimpfwort zum Losungswort. Die Kalvinisten waren außer Rand und Band und zerstörten Hunderte Kirchen. Wie vorauszusehen, ließ sich die schroffe Reaktion Philipps II. nicht lange auf sich warten: 1567 erschien der Herzog von Alva auf dem Plan mit dem Auftrag, gegebenenfalls ein Blutbad anzurichten, um den Aufstand niederzuschlagen. Wilhelm von Oranien, dem Anführer des Widerstandes, gelang es zu entkommen, doch die Grafen von Egmond und von Hoorn wurden verhaftet und mussten alsbald auf dem Marktplatz der Brothalle gegenüber das Schafott besteigen.

Diese ebenso nutzlose wie gehässige Provokation, die mehr Philipp II. als seinem Stellvertreter zuzuschreiben war, wurde das Signal zum offen ausgerufenen Aufstand.

Von den nördlichen Provinzen ausgehend versuchte der umsichtige Prinz von Oranien, die gesamten Niederlande von der spanischen Gewaltherrschaft zu befreien.

Sein Einzug in Brüssel am 23. September 1577 glich einem Triumphzug. Die Frauen knieten vor ihm, als er vorbeizog. Doch blinder Fanatismus schürte die Glut. Eine kalvinistische Minderheit verfolgte die katholische Mehrheit der Brüsseler mit einer Raserei, die den Gewalttätigkeiten der spanischen Soldateska ebenbürtig war. Die Henker beider Parteien zogen am gleichen Strang, und nur Pest und Hungersnot vermochten es, sie an Wirksamkeit zu übertreffen. Man kann deshalb begreifen, dass die Bevölkerung aufatmete, als Alexander Farnese, Herzog von Parma, am 10. März 1585 Brüssel im Auftrag des spanischen Königs zurückeroberte.

Durch die politisch-religiösen Kriege des 16. Jh. brachen die überkommenen siebzehn Provinzen Karls V. auseinander: Im Norden entstanden die kalvinistischen Vereinigten Provinzen, im Süden die katholischen Niederlande.

In den Stürmen, die Brüssel und das Land über sich ergehen lassen mussten, war die Regierungszeit der Erzherzöge Albert und Isabella (1598-1621) wie eine vorübergehende Windstille, eine Atempause, die zwei Jahrzehnte währte. Sie genügte, um Brüssel um zahlreiche Barockkirchen zu bereichern und ihm den Ruf eines Refugiums für verbannte Fürsten einzutragen. Doch schon waren die französischen Truppen im Anzug. Marschall de Villeroi und sein 70.000 Mann starkes Heer hatten den Befehl erhalten, Brüssel um jeden Preis zu erobern. Am 15. August 1695 nahmen ihre achtzehn großkalibrigen Geschütze und ihre fündundzwanzig Mörser die Stadt von der Anhöhe in Scheut aus unter Beschuss. Die Beschießung dauerte sechsunddreißig Stunden. Dreitausend Bomben und zwölfhundert Feuerkugeln gingen über der vom Erzengel Michael beschützten Stadt nieder und verwandelten die Stadtmitte alsbald in ein riesiges Flammenmeer. Obwohl er als Zielscheibe diente, blieb der Turm des Rathauses unversehrt, während im Rathaus selbst Säle mit kostbaren Wandteppichen, berühmten Gemälden und Schätzen in Flammen aufgingen. Das Stadtviertel um den Marktplatz herum glich bald einem großen, schwelenden Schutthaufen. Sechzehn Kirchen, Kapellen und Klöster brannten nieder, und dreitausendachthundert Häuser fielen den Flammen zum Opfer. Doch die Stadt ergab sich nicht. Da keine Feuerkugeln mehr vorhanden waren, beschossen die Brüsseler die Gegner von den Stadtmauern herab mit Pflastersteinen. Schließlich, nachdem die Franzosen vor Namur kapituliert hatten, hob de Villeroi am 5. September die Belagerung auf.

Dem Stadtmagistrat, den Handwerkszünften und einigen Privatpersonen genügten fünf Jahre, um den Marktplatz aus den Trümmern wiedererstehen zu lassen und aus ihm einen der schönsten Plätze der Welt zu machen.

Vom 18. Jh. und der 1715 einsetzenden österreichischen Herrschaft haben die Einwohner Brüssels vor allem den Statthalter Karl von Lothringen in guter Erinnerung behalten. Dieser musikliebende und theaterbesessene Fürst war auch ein Stadtplaner, der seiner Zeit weit voraus war und nach dem Brand des Coudenbergpalasts 1731 den Plan der künftigen Place royale (Königsplatz) vorzeichnete.

1789 nahm Brüssel an der Revolution oder, besser gesagt, an der Konterrevolution Brabants gegen Kaiser Joseph II. teil. Dieser aufklärerische Herrscher versuchte den Verwaltungsapparat der südlichen Niederlande zeitgemäß umzugestalten, jedoch ohne das Volksempfinden vorher auf diesen Umschwung vorbereitet zu haben. Am 11. Januar 1790 wurden die Vereinigten belgischen Staaten in Brüssel aus der Taufe gehoben, doch sowohl innerer Zerfall als auch der Sieg der österreichischen Truppen führten ihr rasches Ende herbei.

Während des folgenden Vierteljahrhunderts war das Schicksal Brüssels eng mit der militärischen und diplomatischen Machtverschiebung in Westeuropa verknüpft : 1792 eroberte es der französische General Dumouriez, 1793 wurde es erneut von den Franzosen eingenommen, 1814 erschienen die Verbündeten auf dem Plan, 1815 erfolgte der Zusammenschluss mit Holland.

Wilhelm I. von Oranien-Nassau, den der Wiener Kongress zum Herrscher über das sogenannte Amalgam Belgiens und Hollands bestimmt hatte, war ein kluger Geschäftsmann und ein unermüdlich tätiger Mensch, doch kein Staatsmann. Gewiss, Brüssel verdankt ihm die Neubelebung seines Handels, seine Sternwarte, seinen botanischen Garten und den neoklassischen Palast des Prinzen van Oranien (jetzt Palast der Akademien), doch wie alle Belgier fühlten sich auch die Einwohner Brüssels als Bürger zweiten Ranges behandelt, denen Presse- und Vereinsfreiheit nicht zugebilligt wurde.

Im August 1830 wurden die Belgier der politischen Fehler Wilhelms I. so überdrüssig, dass sie die von ihm empfangenen materiellen Wohltaten vergaßen und die Holländer aus ihrem Land vertrieben. Die Erhebung begann in Brüssel, als der damals im wörtlichen Sinne tonangebende Tenor La Feuillade im Théâtre de la Monnaie die große Arie der "Stummen von Portici" anstimmte.

Wider Erwarten hatte die Revolution Erfolg. Eine holländische Gegenoffensive wurde im Brüsseler Park abgeschlagen. In den Provinzen folgte man dem Beispiel Brüssels und verjagte die Holländer. So wurde Belgien ein unabhängiges Land mit Brüssel als Hauptstadt. Der Nationale Kongress machte sich sofort an die Arbeit und verankerte die belgische Staatsform, deren eigentlicher Schlussstein die erbliche Monarchie ist, in einem demokratischen Grundgesetz.

Leopold I., der Gründer des belgischen Königshauses, war ein geborener Diplomat. Er verstand es jedoch auch, kluge wirtschaftliche Initiative zu fördern. Am 5. Mai 1835 weihte er in der Nähe der Allée Verte feierlich die erste Eisenbahnstrecke auf dem Kontinent ein. Zu der Eisenbahnstrecke Brüssel-Mechelen kamen in wenigen Jahren viele andere hinzu, so dass Belgien bald über das Verkehrsnetz verfügte, ohne das sein Wohlstand im 19. Jh. wohl undenkbar gewesen wäre.

Leopold II. war nicht nur der Gründer des belgischen Kolonialreichs in Afrika. Sein Beitrag zur städtebaulichen Umgestaltung Brüssels ist unübersehbar. Fast zahllose Verschönerungen der Stadt sind eng mit seinem Namen verknüpft: die Überwölbung der Senne in der Stadtmitte, der Bau der Handelsbörse, der Königlichen Museen der Schönen Künste, des Königpalasts, des Justizpalasts, der anlässlich der Fünfzigjahrfeier der belgischen Unabhängigkeit errichteten Arkaden des Cinquantenaire, die Schaffung der breiten Verkehrsadern in Richtung Tervuren, Laken, Boitsfort, die Anlage der Parks von Forest, Woluwe, Schaerbeek und Laken usw.

Einer witzigen Bemerkung Leon Daudets zufolge gibt es seitdem zwei Städte, die den Namen Brüssel tragen: die Stadt, die Leopold II. bei seinem Regierungsantritt vorfand, und die, welche er bei seinem Hinscheiden hinterließ.

Zweimal, zuerst unter Albert I., dann unter Leopold III., wurde Belgien seiner Neutralität zum Trotz in einen Weltkrieg verstrickt. Beide Male wurde Brüssel durch das deutsche Heer besetzt. In der kurzen Zwischenzeit gelang es Königin Elisabeth, einer großen Mäzenin der Künste, aus der belgischen Hauptstadt einen unumstrittenen Mittelpunkt des internationalen Musiklebens zu machen, indem sie den internationalen Musikwettbewerb Eugène Ysaye ins Leben rief. Auch unter König Bauduin erfüllte Brüssel diese Mission mit Erfolg.

Bereits als Prinz von Lüttich nahm König Albert II. regen Anteil an der Entwicklung der Stadt und setzte sich für die Instandhaltung ihrer Baudenkmäler ein. Nicht des Ehrentitels halber wurde er Ehrenpräsident des Komitees "Quartier des Arts"; in diesem Amt gelang es ihm wiederholt, in entscheidendem Maße auf die Stadtplanung einzuwirken.

Brüssel war früher eine Hauptstadt mit provinziellem Anstrich. Seine jeglicher Form städtischer Überheblichkeit baren Bürger pflegten eher eine übertriebene Bescheidenheit an den Tag zu legen. Dies ist auch heute noch so. Deshalb war es immer und ist es auch heute noch eine von weltoffener Toleranz geprägte Stadt. Seit es Hauptsitz der Verwaltungsorgane der Europäischen Gemeinschaft ist, "schätzen die zwölftausend dort verweilenden internationalen Beamten die jeder Beschreibung spottende, ungewohnte und unvorhersehbare Weise, auf die es Banalität und Überraschung, alltägliches Einerlei und weltstädtische Vielseitigkeit miteinander verbindet, ja, zugleich Weltpolitik treibt und unbeirrbar seine Rolle als Hauptstadt eines kleinen Pufferstaats weiterspielt" (J. De Decker).

Seitdem sich auch die NATO in einer der Gemeinden Brüssels angesiedelt hat, ist Brüssel die einzige Hauptstadt der Welt, die ein dreifaches diplomatisches Korps beherbergt: ein beim König und dessen Regierung, ein bei der Europäischen Gemeinschaft und ein bei der NATO akkreditiertes.

Die großen, von den jeweiligen Regierungen unabhängigen Organisationen haben sich diesem Trend angeschlossen. Mehr als fünfhundert dieser Interessengemeinschaften und -gruppen sind in Brüssel vertreten. Diese Zahl liegt zwar etwas unter der für Paris zutreffenden, doch in dieser Hinsicht hat Brüssel bereits London, Genf und New-York hinter sich gelassen.

Zweifelsohne fühlen sich Wirtschaftsleben und Finanzwelt immer stärker zum leicht zugänglichen, dienstbereiten und gastfreundlichen Mittelpunkt hingezogen, in dem Europas Zukunft Gestalt gewinnt.

À quelques pas du «Berlaymont», siège emblématique de l'Union européenne édifié en 1970 et récemment rénové, la rue Archimède débouche sur un espace verdoyant : l'enfilade des **squares Marie-Louise** *(photo)*, Marguerite et Ambiorix. Tous trois sont bordés de maisons en majorité du début du XXᵉ siècle. Au milieu des pelouses et parmi les sentiers sont dressées des sculptures des meilleurs artistes de ce temps : Constantin Meunier, Jef Lambeaux et Victor Rousseau.

À l'avènement du roi Léopold II en 1865, Bruxelles comptait 250.000 habitants; à sa mort en 1909, elle en avait 800.000. Cet accroissement démographique alla de pair avec le développement de la construction. C'est dans ce contexte que se situent les quelques 1500 habitations édifiées en un style à dominante Art Nouveau entre 1893 et 1910.

A short walk along the Rue Archimède from the "Berlaymont", the symbolic seat of the European Union built in 1970 and recently renovated, is a green space composed of a series of parks : the **squares Marie-Louise** *(photo)*, Marguerite and Ambiorix. All three are lined with houses, mostly from the early 20th century. In the middle of the lawns and along the paths stand sculptures by the leading artists of the period : Constantin Meunier, Jef Lambeaux and Victor Rousseau.

When King Leopold II acceded to the throne in 1865 Brussels had 250,000 inhabitants. When he died in 1909 there were 800,000. Construction grew along with the population. Within this context some 1500 houses were built in a predominantly Art Nouveau style.

Op enkele passen van het Berlaymontgebouw, symbolische zetel van de Europese Unie, gebouwd in 1970 en onlangs gerenoveerd, ligt de Archimedesstraat, die uitloopt op een groene oase : achtereenvolgens vindt men er de **Maria-Louizasquare** *(foto)*, de Margarethasquare en de Ambiorixsquare. De drie pleinen worden overwegend omzoomd door huizen uit het begin van de 20ste eeuw. Midden op de grasvelden en in de paden staan beeldhouwwerken van de beste kunstenaars uit die tijd: Constantin Meunier, Jef Lambeaux en Victor Rousseau.

Bij de troonsbestijging van koning Leopold II in 1865 telde Brussel 250.000 inwoners; bij zijn overlijden in 1909 waren het er 800.000. Deze bevolkingsaangroei ging gepaard met een ontwikkeling van de bouwnijverheid. In deze context situeren zich de ongeveer 1500 woningen die tussen 1893 en 1910 werden opgetrokken in Art Nouveau stijl.

Wenige Schritte von "Berlaymont", dem im Jahre 1970 erbauten und kürzlich renovierten sinnbildlichen Sitz der Europäischen Union entfernt, mündet die Rue Archimède in eine Grünfläche: die miteinander verbundenen **Squares Marie-Louise** *(Foto)*, Marguerite und Ambiorix. Alle drei werden von in der Mehrzahl Anfang des 20. Jahrhunderts erbauten Häusern gesäumt. In der Mitte der Rasenflächen und zwischen den Wegen stehen Skulpturen der herausragendsten Künstler jener Zeit: Constantin Meunier, Jef Lambeaux und Victor Rousseau.

Bei der Thronbesteigung König Leopolds II. im Jahre 1865 zählte Brüssel 250.000 Einwohner, bei seinem Tod im Jahre 1909 waren es bereits 800.000. Dieses demografische Wachstum ging mit der baulichen Fortentwicklung einher. So wurden im Zeitraum von 1893 bis 1910 rund 1500 Wohnungen in einem vom Art nouveau dominierten Stil errichtet.

Depuis 1992, Bruxelles ne partage pas seulement avec Strasbourg les sessions du **Parlement européen**, elle est aussi le siège de toutes les autres réunions et activités parlementaires. Ce privilège impliquait la construction d'un ensemble de bâtiments pouvant abriter les travaux des 626 députés représentant 372 millions de citoyens. Situé derrière la petite gare Léopold, entre la place du Luxembourg et la rue Wiertz, le complexe de 372.000 m² abrite le vaste hémicycle parlementaire ainsi que 2600 bureaux et 78 salles de conférence.

(Page 23 ci-contre)
Au pied du restaurant des députés et des fonctionnaires européens, vaste éventail de verre sous une voûte de même composition, s'étale un panorama de la ville dans l'axe de la rue du Luxembourg.

Sinds 1992 herbergt Brussel niet enkel de zittingen van het **Europees Parlement** – samen met Straatsburg – maar ook alle andere parlementaire zittingen en activiteiten. Dit voorrecht impliceerde wel het bouwen van kantoren die plaats bieden aan 626 afgevaardigden die 372 miljoen burgers vertegenwoordigen. Dit 372.000 m² grote complex situeert zich achter het kleine Leopoldstation, tussen het Luxemburgplein en de Wiertzstraat, het omvat het grote parlementaire halfrond, 2600 kantoren en 78 vergaderzalen.

(Bladzijde 23 hier tegenover)
Het restaurant van de Europese afgevaardigden en ambtenaren lijkt een grote glazen waaier onder een gewelf van dezelfde samenstelling. Aan de voet van het restaurant, in het verlengde van de Luxemburgstraat, strekt zich een panorama van de stad uit.

Since 1992 Brussels not only has shared with Strasbourg the sessions of the **European Parliament** but has also become the seat of other meetings and parliamentary activities. This privilege necessitated the construction of a group of buildings to house the work of the 626 representatives of 372 million citizens. The 372,000 square meter complex behind the little Leopold station, between the Place du Luxembourg and Rue Wiertz, contains the huge parliamentary hemicycle as well as 2600 offices and 78 conference rooms.

(Page 23 opposite)
A panorama of the city on the axis of the Rue du Luxembourg can be seen stretching out beneath the restaurant for members and bureaucrats through a large glass fan under glass vaulting.

Seit 1992 finden in Brüssel im Wechsel mit Straßburg nicht nur die Sitzungswochen des **Europäischen Parlaments** statt, die Stadt ist auch der Ort aller anderen parlamentarischen Versammlungen und Tätigkeiten. Dieses Privileg schloss den Bau einer Gebäudegruppe zur Unterbringung aller Arbeitsplätze der 626 Abgeordneten als Vertreter von 372 Millionen Bürger mit ein. Der 372.000 m² große Komplex hinter dem kleinen Leopold-Bahnhof zwischen der Place du Luxembourg und der Rue Wiertz umfasst das große Halbrund des Plenarsaals sowie 2600 Büros und 78 Sitzungssäle.

(Nebenstehende Seite 23)
Zu Füßen des Restaurants der europäischen Abgeordneten und Beamten, einem riesigen Fächer aus Glas unter einem Gewölbe gleicher Gliederung, eröffnet sich in der Achse der Rue du Luxembourg das Bild der Stadt.

(Photo panoramique précédente)

Sous le règne de Léopold II, l'aristocratie et la grande bourgeoisie bruxelloises se fixaient volontiers au nouveau quartier Léopold dont la construction s'était développée à la faveur du prolongement de la rue de la Loi.

Plusieurs établissements sont éparpillés au sein ou en lisière du **parc Léopold**, le long de la rue Belliard. De gauche à droite, l'institut des Sciences naturelles dont le musée est célèbre pour ses iguanodons trouvés à Bernissart en 1878, la bibliothèque de l'ancien institut de sociologie fondé par Ernest Solvay en 1901, le lycée Emile Jacqmain (1893) et l'institut dentaire George Eastman (1935). Mais le destin de capitale européenne a totalement transformé le quartier par la construction de l'ambitieux bâtiment du Parlement européen. Par sa dimension et son audace architecturale, l'édifice a impressionné les Bruxellois qui, d'emblée, l'ont surnommé le *Caprice des dieux*.

(Vorige panoramische foto)

Tijdens de heerschappij van Leopold II planden de Brusselse aristocratie en bourgeoisie met graagte een nieuwe Leopoldwijk, die voor zijn opbouw profiteerde van de verlenging van de Wetstraat.

Verscheidene gebouwen liggen verspreid in en rond het **Leopoldpark**, langs de Belliardstraat. Van links naar rechts, het Instituut voor Natuurwetenschappen, waarvan het museum bekendheid geniet omwille van de iguanodons die in 1878 in Bernissart werden gevonden, de bibliotheek van het oude Instituut voor Sociologie, gesticht door Ernest Solvay in 1901, het lyceum Emile Jacqmain (1893) en het tandheelkundig instituut George Eastman (1935). De bestemming als Europese hoofdstad heeft deze wijk helemaal veranderd door de constructie van het ambitieuze gebouw van het Europees Parlement. Door zijn afmetingen en zijn gewaagde architectuur heeft het gebouw een grote indruk gemaakt op de Brusselaars, die het onmiddellijk bedachten met de bijnaam *Caprice des dieux*.

(Preceding panoramic photo)

During the reign of Leopold II the aristocracy and upper classes were pleased to settle in the new Leopold quarter developed around the extension of Rue de la Loi.

A number of establishments are sprinkled in the **Leopold Park** or on its edge on Rue Belliard. From left to right are the Natural History Museum renowned for its iguanodons found at Bernissart in 1878, the former library of the Sociological Institute founded by Ernest Solvay in 1901, the Emile Jacqmain school of 1893 and the George Eastman Dental Institute of 1935. The new destiny as European capital has completely transformed the quarter, however, by the construction of the ambitious European Parliament building. The size and architectural audacity of the building so impressed the people of Brussels that they immediately nicknamed it *Caprice des dieux* – "Whim of the Gods".

(Voranstehendes Panoramafoto)

Unter der Herrschaft von Leopold II. ließen sich die Aristo-kratie und das Großbürgertum von Brüssel gerne in dem neuen Leopold-Viertel nieder, das sich über eine Verlängerung der Rue de la Loi ausgedehnt hatte.

Im oder am Rand des **Leopoldparks** entlang der Rue Belliard liegen verstreut mehrere Einrichtungen. Von links nach rechts das Naturwissenschaftliche Institut, dessen Museum für seine in Bernissart im Jahre 1878 gefundenen Iguanodone berühmt ist, die Bibliothek des von Ernest Solvay im Jahre 1901 gegründeten alten Soziologischen Instituts, das Lycée Emile Jacqmain (1893) sowie das zahnmedizinische Institut George Eastman (1935). Aber die Bestimmung als europäische Hauptstadt hat das Viertel durch den Bau der gewaltigen Anlage des Europäischen Parlaments vollkommen verändert. Die Brüsseler zeigten sich durch die Dimension und architektonische Kühnheit dieses Gebäudes beeindruckt und gaben ihm sogleich den Beinamen *Caprice des dieux* ("Laune der Götter").

△

Antoine Wiertz, qui avait obtenu le grand prix de Rome pour une toile conçue selon les recettes du classicisme, se convertit ensuite à la manière de Rubens mais il n'eut aucun succès au salon de Paris de 1839. Il partagea alors son temps entre des portraits – il en est d'excellents – et d'immenses compositions lyrico-décoratives. En 1850, ayant offert au gouvernement une part importante de son œuvre, il obtint en échange la construction d'un vaste atelier à la mesure de ses ambitions – aujourd'hui le **musée Wiertz**. Il passa les dernières années de sa vie dans la maison bourgeoise qui jouxte cet atelier, rue Vautier, et ne tarda pas à sombrer dans une névrose très proche de la folie.

Antoine Wiertz, who won the Grand Prize of Rome for a strictly classical painting, later converted to the style of Rubens but had no success at the Paris Salon of 1839. He then devoted his time to painting portraits, some of which are excellent, and enormous lyrically decorative compositions. In 1850 he offered a large part of his work to the State, receiving in exchange a huge studio, built to the scale of his ambitions and which is today the **Wiertz Museum**. He spent the last years of his life in a comfortable house adjoining this studio on Rue Vautier and quickly sank into a neurotic state close to madness.

Antoon Wiertz had de grote prijs van Rome behaald voor een doek in classicistische stijl. Toen hij later de stijl van Rubens begon na te bootsen, had hij op het salon in Parijs in 1839 hoegenaamd geen succes meer. Van toen af wijdde hij zich helemaal aan een dubbele taak : het schilderen van portretten – sommige zijn echte meesterwerken – en van grandioze, lyrisch-decoratieve composities. ln 1850 schonk hij een groot deel van zijn œuvre aan de Belgische Staat. In ruil daarvoor werd hem een ruim atelier aangeboden waarin hij zijn ambitieuze dromen gestalte kon geven; het huidige **Wiertzmuseum**. Zijn laatste levensjaren woonde hij in het aanpalende herenhuis in de Vautierstraat, maar werd hoe langer hoe heviger heen en weer geslingerd tussen waanzin en zenuwinzinkingen.

Anton Wiertz hatte für ein Gemälde nach klassizistischem Rezept den großen Preis von Rom erhalten. Als er später Rubens nachzueifern begann, stieß er 1839 auf schroffe Ablehnung in Paris. Seitdem arbeitete er als oft meisterhafter Porträtist, vor allem jedoch als Maler monumentaler lyrisch-dekorativer Kompositionen. Als er 1850 der belgischen Regierung den größten Teil seiner Werke angeboten hatte, erhielt er, sozusagen als Entgelt, ein geräumiges Atelier, das seinen ehrgeizigen Plänen entsprach. Dieses Atelier ist jetzt das **Wiertzmuseum**. Während seiner letzten Lebensjahre wohnte er fast nebenan, in einem Herrenhaus in der Rue Vautier. Diese Jahre wurden jedoch bald zu einer qualvollen Gratwanderung an der Grenze zwischen Nervenzusammenbruch und Wahnsinn.

▷

Durant la seconde moitié du XIXᵉ siècle, la valeur des terrains avait plus que décuplé dans le centre de la ville. Il en résulta la construction d'habitations privées de plus en plus nombreuses dans la proche périphérie jusqu'alors épargnée par la spéculation. Les maisons de la **rue Vautier** appartiennent à cette époque. Chacune d'entre elles, prise isolément, n'a rien de très original sinon le jardinet grillagé, les hautes fenêtres gracieusement encadrées et les balcons qui témoignent d'une certaine aisance bourgeoise. Mais c'est l'ensemble de ces maisons, toutes semblables, qui séduit le regard. L'individualisme des constructeurs a cédé ici devant le désir de cohérence et d'harmonie.

During the second half of the 19th century land prices in the downtown area rose sharply, leading to more and more private homes being built on the outskirts where land had not yet been bought up by speculators. The houses on **Rue Vautier** date from this period. Taken individually none of these houses is very original except for details such as a tiny, fenced garden, tall gracefully framed windows or balconies, evidence of a certain middle-class prosperity. All the same, this ensemble of similar houses is pleasing to the eye. It is very rare in Brussels to see the individualism of the builders bow before the desire for consistency and harmony.

Tussen 1850 en 1900 is de prijs voor bouwgrond in het centrum van Brussel vertienvoudigd. Daarom werden er meer en meer privéwoningen aan de rand van de stad gebouwd, waar grondspeculatie haast nog een onbekend verschijnsel was. De huizen in de **Vautierstraat** dateren uit die periode. De voortuintjes met traliehekken, de hoge, netjes omkaderde ramen en balkons getuigen van kleinburgerlijke welgesteldheid, maar ook van een totaal gebrek aan originaliteit. Deze huizen zijn precies eender en het verwoede individualisme dat de Brusselse bouwlustigen vaak heel terecht wordt verweten, heeft hier de vlag gestreken voor het verlangen om op te gaan in een groter harmonisch geheel.

Zwischen 1850 und 1900 stieg der Preis für Bauplätze im Stadtzentrum um das Zehnfache. Deshalb wurden immer mehr Privathäuser am damaligen Stadtrand gebaut, der von der Grundspekulation verschont geblieben war. In dieser Zeit entstanden die hier gezeigten Häuser in der **Rue Vautier**. In baukundlicher Hinsicht bekunden die vergitterten Vorgärten, die hohen Fenster mit ihren schmucken Einfassungen und die Balkone zwar einen beschränkten bürgerlichen Wohlstand, doch ihnen fehlt jede Spur von Originalität. Schaut man sich die Häuser an, dann sieht man, wie sehr sie einander gleichen. Statt des den Brüsseler Bauherren oft zu Recht vorgeworfenen übertriebenen Individualismus überwiegt hier entschieden die Einordnung in ein ausgewogenes, harmonisches Ganzes.

△▷

Une *warande* ou garenne jouxtait l'ancien palais ducal du Coudenberg, incendié en 1731. Il fut décidé, sous le gouvernement de Marie-Thérèse, d'y créer un parc classique, d'une parfaite symétrie mais animé de statues, de bassins et de bosquets : le **parc de Bruxelles**. Ses allées ménagent de belles perspectives vers le **Palais de la Nation**, siège de la Chambre des Représentants, achevé en 1783. Près du petit bassin octogonal, la «Fillette à la Coquille» est l'œuvre gracieuse et sans prétention d'Alphonse de Tombay.

In de omgeving van het voormalige hertogelijk paleis op de Coudenberg, dat in 1731 in vlammen opging, bevond zich een warande. Tijdens de regering van Maria-Theresia besliste men hiervan een volmaakt symmetrisch park te maken met standbeelden, vijvers en bosschages: het **Park van Brussel**. De hoofdlanen geven een prachtig uitzicht op het **Paleis der Natie** – nu de Kamer van Volksvertegenwoordigers – dat in 1783 voltooid werd. Het "Meisje met de schelp" vlak bij het kleine, achthoekige bekken is een bekoorlijk zij het ook pretentieloos werk van Alphonse de Tombay.

A *warande* – a game enclosure – adjoined the ducal palace of Coudenberg which burned down in 1731. Under the government of Maria Theresa it was turned into a classical park, perfectly symmetrical and decorated with statuary, ponds and copses : the **park of Brussels**. The paths were designed to afford a view of the **Palace of the Nation**, seat of the Parliament, completed in 1783. The charmingly simple "Girl With a Shell" near the octagonal basin is a work of Alphonse de Tombay.

Neben dem herzoglichen Schloss am Coudenberg, das 1731 einem Brand zum Opfer fiel, befand sich ein Wildgehege. Während der Herrschaft Maria Theresias wurde beschlossen, dort einen klassizistischen, völlig symmetrischen Park mit Statuen, Wasserbecken und Lustwäldchen anzulegen, der **Park von Brüssel**. Die Alleen gewähren schöne Ausblicke auf den Königspalast und den 1783 vollendeten **Palast der Nation**, in dem nun die Kammer der Abgeordnenten ihren Sitz hat. Beim kleinen, achteckigen Becken erhebt sich heute noch das "Mädchen mit der Muschel", ein anmutiges und zugleich schlichtes Werk von Alphonse de Tombay.

(Pages 28 à 31)

Léopold II aimait la rigueur classique du style Louis XVI. Celui-ci domine dans la façade du **Palais royal**, telle qu'elle fut transformée par l'architecte français Maquet à partir de 1904. Les trois avant-corps reliés par deux ailes assurent une ordonnance majestueuse qu'accentuent la double colonnade du corps central, le fronton triangulaire orné d'un bas-relief de Thomas Vinçotte et le dôme.

Le caractère grandiose de la Salle du Trône *(à droite)* doit beaucoup à la courbe des arcs et au plafond voûté. Comme dans la Salle Empire *(à gauche)*, les colonnes cannelées du XVIIIe siècle y ont été maintenues.

(Blz. 28 tot 31)

Leopold II was erg gesteld op de klassieke soberheid van de Lodewijk XVI-stijl. Deze bepaalt dan ook de voorkant van het **Koninklijk Paleis**, dat hij vanaf 1904 door de Franse architect Maquet liet herbouwen. De drie door vleugelvormige overgangen met elkaar verbonden voorgebouwen verlenen aan het geheel een nogal majestueuze aanblik, die nog onderstreept wordt door de dubbele zuilenrij van de centrale uitbouw, de geveldriehoek met het bas-reliëf van Thomas Vinçotte en de koepel.

De indrukwekkende grootsheid van de Troonzaal *(rechts)* is hoofdzakelijk te danken aan het overwelfde plafond en de vorm van de gewelfbogen. Zoals in de Empire-Zaal *(links)* zijn ook hier de 18de-eeuwse geribde zuilen gespaard gebleven.

(Pages 28 to 31)

Leopold II admired the strict classicism of the Louis XVI style which dominates the facade of the **Royal Palace**, remodelled by the French architect Maquet in 1904. The three bays of the façade are linked by two wings in a majestic sweep which is accented by the double colonnade of the central bay, the triangular pediment with a low relief by Thomas Vinçotte and the dome.

The arches and vaulted ceiling contribute to the imposing feeling of the Throne Room *(right)* where one finds the same 18th century fluted columns as in the Empire Room *(left)*.

(S. 28 bis 31)

König Leopold II. bewunderte die klassische Strenge des Louis-seize. Von ihr wird die Vorderseite des **Königspalastes** geprägt, den er 1904 vom französischen Architekten Maquet umbauen ließ. Die drei durch flügelartige Übergänge miteinander verbundenen Vorsprünge verleihen dem Ganzen ein majestätisches Aussehen, das noch durch die doppelte Säulenreihe des Mittelteils, durch das mit einem Basrelief von Thomas Vinçotte geschmückte Giebeldreieck und durch die Kuppel verstärkt wird. Der Schwung der Bögen sowie das Deckengewölbe tragen zur grandiosen Pracht des Thronsaales *(rechts)* bei. Wie im Empiresaal *(links)* wurden auch hier die kannelierten Säulen aus dem 18. Jh. beibehalten.

△▷
L'hôtel de maître à l'angle de la rue Royale et de la place des Palais fut édifié par l'architecte Guimard en 1779. Léo Errera l'acquit en 1868.

Depuis 1992, **l'hôtel Errera** appartient à la Communauté flamande qui l'a sauvé de son abandon. Le style Louis XVI de l'intérieur a été conservé dans les salons parquetés et lambrissés. Un des salons du 1er étage est tapissé de papiers-peints chinois.

Het herenhuis op de hoek van de Koningsstraat en het Paleizenplein werd gebouwd in 1779 door architect Guimard. Léo Errera verwierf het in 1868.

Sinds 1992 behoort het **Huis Errera** toe aan de Vlaamse Gemeenschap, die het pand redde van verwaarlozing. De Lodewijk XVI-stijl van het interieur is bewaard gebleven in de met parket en lambrizering aangeklede salons. Eén van de salons op de 1ste verdieping is behangen met Chinees behangpapier.

The mansion on the corner of Rue Royale and Place des Palais was built by the architect Guimard in 1779. Léo Errera bought it in 1868.

The **Errera Mansion** has belonged to the Flemish Community since 1992, thus saving it from abandon. The Louis XVI style of the interior has been retained in the parquet floored, wainscoted reception rooms. One on the first floor is hung with Chinese wallpaper.

Das herrschaftliche Stadthaus an der Ecke der Rue Royale und der Place des Palais wurde 1779 von Architekt Guimard erbaut. Léo Errera erwarb es im Jahre 1868.

Seit 1992 gehört das **Herrenhaus Errera** der flämischen Gemeinschaft, die es vor dem Verfall gerettet hat. Der Louis-seize-Stil im Inneren wurde in den mit Parkett ausgelegten und getäfelten Salons bewahrt. Einer der Salons im 1. Stockwerk ist mit chinesischer Tapete verkleidet.

◁◁

Dominant le quadrilatère de la **Place Royale** créée par Charles de Lorraine en style Louis XVI, l'**église Saint-Jacques sur Coudenberg** (1776-1787) évoque les temples gréco-romains. Est-ce pour ce motif qu'elle devint Temple de la Raison puis Temple de la Loi sous l'occupation française?

The **church of St. James-on-Coudenberg** (1776-1787) which resembles a Greco-Roman temple dominates the **Place Royale** commissioned by the Austrian governor Charles of Lorraine in the style of Louis XVI. Perhaps that is why, under the French occupation, it first became the Temple of Reason and then the Temple of Law.

Het vierkante plein in Lodewijk XVI-stijl, het **Koningsplein**, is een realisatie van Karel van Lorreinen. Het wordt beheerst door de **Sint-Jacobskerk op Coudenberg** (1776-1787) die herinnert aan de Grieks-Romeinse tempels. Misschien is het wel om die reden dat zij tijdens de Franse bezetting eerst Tempel van de Rede en daarna Tempel van de Wet werd.

Die **Kirche Saint-Jacques sur Coudenberg** (1776-1787), die das von Karl von Lothringen im Louis-XVI-Stil geschaffene Viereck der **Place Royale** überragt, erinnert an griechisch-römische Tempel. Vielleicht wurde sie aus diesem Grunde unter französischer Herrschaft zum Tempel der Vernunft und später zum Tempel des Gesetzes umfunktioniert.

◁△
Dans la nuit du 3 au 4 février 1731, sur la colline du Coudenberg, le palais des ducs de Bourgogne, l'un des plus vastes et prestigieux monuments civils de toute l'Europe, fut entièrement détruit par le feu. Quarante ans plus tard, on décréta enfin de niveler le site resté à l'état de décombres et d'y créer une place symétrique. Les fouilles récentes dans les **souterrains du palais du Coudenberg**, sous le niveau de la place Royale, ont permis de dégager d'importants vestiges très évocateurs. Parmi ceux-ci, l'ancienne rue Isabelle _(à gauche)_ tracée vers 1660 sur ordre de l'archiduchesse puis supprimée et couverte d'une voûte au XVIIIe siècle. Plus intéressantes encore apparaissent les caves près de l'actuel musée Belle-Vue, demeurées quasi intactes _(à droite)_.

The palace of the Dukes of Burgundy on the Coudenberg hill, one of the largest and most renowned monuments in all of Europe, was completely destroyed by fire the night of February 3-4, 1731. Forty years later it was finally decreed that the ruins be razed and replaced by a symmetrical square. Recent excavations of the **lower level of the palace of Coudenberg** lying under Place Royale have discovered considerable and very evocative remains. Among them is the former Isabelle Street _(left)_ made in 1660 by command of the Archduchess and later closed and vaulted over in the 18th century. Even more interesting are the cellars near the present Belle-Vue Museum which are largely intact _(right)_.

In de nacht van 3 op 4 februari 1731 vernielde een brand één van de grootste en meest prestigieuze burgermonumenten van Europa, het paleis van de hertogen van Bourgondië op de Coudenberg. Veertig jaar later werd eindelijk besloten om de puinresten op te ruimen en een symmetrisch plein aan te leggen. De recente opgravingen in de **onderaardse gewelven van het Coudenbergpaleis**, onder het Koningsplein, legden belangrijke resten bloot die nog steeds tot de verbeelding spreken. Eén ervan is de voormalige Isabellastraat _(links)_ die rond 1660 werd aangelegd op bevel van de aartshertogin, en daarna met een gewelf werd overtrokken. Nog interessanter zijn de kelders bij het huidige Belle-Vue museum, die zo goed als intact zijn gebleven _(rechts)_.

In der Nacht vom 3. auf 4. Februar 1731 wurde auf dem Hügel des Coudenberg der Palast der Herzöge von Burgund, eines der größten und kostbarsten zivilen Bauwerke Europas, vom Feuer völlig zerstört. Vierzig Jahre später ordnete man schließlich an, die noch immer in Ruinen liegende Stätte einzuebnen und einen symmetrischen Platz zu schaffen. Bei kürzlich im **Untergrund des Coudenberg-Palastes** auf der Höhe der Place Royale durchgeführten Grabungen, konnten bedeutende Überreste freigelegt werden, die weitreichende Aufschlüsse geben. Unter ihnen die ehemalige Rue Isabelle _(links)_, die um das Jahr 1660 im Auftrag der Erzherzogin angelegt worden war und im 18. Jh. ihrer Funktion enthoben und mit einem Gewölbe bedeckt wurde. Noch interessanter sind die beinahe intakt gebliebenen Keller in der Nähe des heutigen Belle-Vue Museums _(rechts)_.

Prince jovial et bon vivant, Charles de Lorraine conquit aisément l'affection des Bruxellois. Animée de nombreux bas-reliefs et statues, la façade du **Palais de Charles de Lorraine** reprend, dans le style Louis XVI autrichien, les thèmes antiques avec une exquise élégance. Le Musée d'Art Moderne s'ouvre dans le sous-sol de la cour, aujourd'hui place du Musée, et préserve donc l'environnement architectural du XVIIIᵉ siècle. Un grand puits vitré assure l'éclairage *a giorno* d'une partie de ses salles.

Au pied de l'escalier du Palais de Charles de Lorraine, qu'empruntaient les francs-maçons de la loge Saint-Charles, l'Hercule en marbre blanc, sculpté par Laurent Delvaux en 1770, symbolisait l'idéal du maître de céans. Parfois guerrier, le bon duc était aussi alchimiste en quête de la pierre philosophale, un travail d'Hercule...

(Page 39)

La grande salle en rotonde du palais, du plus pur style Louis XVI, est décorée de trophées et de guirlandes en stuc. La coupole posée sur les colonnes doriques est d'une telle hardiesse que certains, lors de la construction, doutèrent de sa solidité. Ils sous-estimaient le talent de l'architecte Laurent-Benoît Dewez.

Karel van Lorreinen was een joviale en vrolijke levensgenieter die de weg naar het hart van de Brusselaars wist te vinden. Op de gevel van het **Paleis van Karel van Lorreinen**, opgetrokken in Oostenrijkse Lodewijk XVI-stijl, worden thema's uit de Oudheid zeer levendig weergegeven in vele bas-reliëfs en beelden. Het Museum voor Moderne Kunst strekt zich uit onder het huidige Museumplein, waarvan het historische kader en de 18de-eeuwse stijl bijgevolg onaangetast zijn gebleven. Dankzij de grote, half-ovale, diep uitgegraven lichtput of lichtkoker hebben de zalen ten dele *a giorno* verlichting.

Aan de voet van de trap, waarlangs de vrijmetselaars van de loge Sint-Carolus zich naar hun verenigingslokaal begaven, staat een witmarmeren Hercules van Laurent Delvaux (1770), die het levensideaal van de heer des huizes belichaamt. De soms krijgslustige hertog was ook een alchimist op zoek naar de steen der wijzen, een echte herculesarbeid...

(Bladzijde 39)

De grote ronde zaal van het paleis, in een zeer zuivere Lodewijk XVI-stijl, is versierd met trofeeën en bloemslingers in stucwerk. De koepel die op de dorische zuilen rust is zo gewaagd dat, tijdens de bouwwerken, sommigen twijfelden aan de soliditeit. Zij onderschatten het talent van architect Laurent-Benoît Dewez.

Charles of Lorraine, a jovial prince who liked to enjoy life, soon gained the affection of the people of Brussels. Decorated with numerous carvings in low relief and with statues, the façade of the **Palace of Charles of Lorraine** is an exquisite rendering of subjects from classical antiquity in the elegant Austrian style of 18th century architecture. The Museum of Modern Art is built under the Place du Musée, thus preserving the architectural harmony of the 18th century square. Some of the rooms are illuminated by daylight, provided by a large countersunk glass wall.

In the Palace of Charles of Lorraine a white marble Hercules, sculpted by Laurent Delvaux in 1770, stands at the foot of the staircase formerly used by the Freemasons of the St. Charles Lodge. He symbolized the ideals of the master of the house, for the good Duke was not only a soldier but also an alchemist, seeking the Philosopher's Stone, a true labour of Hercules!

(Page 39)

The great rotunda of the palace is in the purest Louis XVI style, decorated with trophies and garlands in stucco. The cupola poised on Doric columns is so daring that some feared for its stability during its construction but they underestimated the talent of Laurent-Benoît Dewez, the architect.

Karl von Lothringen, ein jovialer und lebenslustiger Prinz, erwarb sich rasch die Zuneigung der Brüsseler. Die Fassade des im österreichischen Louis XVI-Stil erbauten **Palais Karls von Lothringen** zeigt zahlreiche antiken Themen nachempfundene Flachreliefs und Statuen von ausgesuchter Formschönheit. Die Säle des Museums für moderne Kunst breiten sich unter der Place du Musée aus, so dass die architektonische Einheit des im Stil des 18. Jh. angelegten Platzes völlig unangetastet blieb. Der tief in die Erde eindringende Lichtkegel in der Form eines halben Ovals lässt in die meisten Säle natürliches Licht von oft verblüffender Helligkeit hineinströmen.

Am Fuß der Treppe, auf der die Freimaurer der Loge Saint Charles zu ihrem Versammlungsort schritten, steht eine Statue des Herkules aus weißem Marmor. Dieses Werk von Laurent Delvaux (1770) zeugt vom Lebensideal des Fürsten, der Kriegsabenteuer zwar nicht verabscheute, sich jedoch als Alchimist einer anderen Herkulesarbeit widmete, nämlich der Suche nach dem Stein der Weisen.

(Seite 39)

Der große, runde Saal des Palais in reinstem Louis-seize-Stil ist mit Trophäen und Girlanden aus Stuck verziert. Die auf dorischen Säulen ruhende Kuppel ist von solch kühner Architektur, dass einige beim Bau um ihre Stabilität fürchteten. Sie unterschätzten das Talent des Architekten Laurent-Benoît Dewez.

△
Initialement palais des beaux-arts destinés aux salons et expositions artistiques, le **musée d'Art ancien** – l'un des très riches Musées royaux des Beaux-arts de Bruxelles – fut inauguré en 1880. Sa façade de style éclectique avec dominante classique fut érigée d'après le projet d'Alphonse Balat.

Het **Museum voor Oudheidkunde**, één van de drie bijzonder rijke Koninklijke Musea voor Schone Kunsten in Brussel, werd ingehuldigd in 1880 en was oorspronkelijk bestemd voor kunsttentoonstellingen en salons. De voorgevel in vooral klassieke eclectische stijl werd gebouwd volgens het project van Alphonse Balat.

Initially conceived as a venue for art exhibitions and shows the **Museum of Antique Fine Art** – one of the richest of the Royal Museums in Brussels – was opened in 1880. Its eclectic façade dominated by neoclassical was constructed to designs by Alphonse Balat.

Im ursprünglichen, für Kunstmessen und Ausstellungen bestimmten Palais der Schönen Künste wurde im Jahre 1880 das **Museum für Alte Kunst** – eines der sehr reich ausgestatteten Königlichen Kunstmuseen von Brüssel – eingeweiht. Seine Fassade in eklektizistischem Stil mit klassizistischer Dominante wurde nach dem Entwurf von Alphonse Balat gestaltet.

▷
Le belvédère du nouveau musée des Instruments de musique domine les jardins du **Mont des Arts**, récemment redessinés par René Pechère. À ses pieds la statue équestre du roi Albert Iᵉʳ fait face à une rangée de maisons modernes édifiées dans le style du XVIIᵉ siècle; elles forment l'avant-plan d'un panorama où s'impose, dans toute son élégance, la tour blanche de l'hôtel de ville.

De uitkijktoren van het nieuwe museum van Muziekinstrumenten overheerst de tuinen van de **Kunstberg**, die recent werden herontworpen door René Pechère. Aan de voet van de Kunstberg staat het ruiterstandbeeld van koning Albert I, dat uitkijkt over een rij moderne huizen gebouwd in de stijl van de 17de eeuw; zij vormen de voorgrond van een panorama waarin de witte toren van het stadhuis in al zijn elegantie opvalt.

The belvedere of the new Museum of Musical Instruments dominates the gardens of the **Mont des Arts**, recently redesigned by René Pechère. The equestrian statue of King Albert I at the bottom of the gardens faces a row of modern houses built in the style of the 17th century. They form the foreground of a panorama dominated by the elegant white tower of the City Hall.

Die Aussichtsterrasse des neuen Musikinstrumentenmuseums erhebt sich über den Gärten des **Kunstbergs**, die kürzlich von René Pechère neu gestaltet wurden. An ihrem unteren Ende steht die Reiterstatue von König Albert I. gegenüber einer Reihe moderner Häuser, die im Stil des 17. Jahrhunderts errichtet wurden; sie bilden den Vordergrund eines Panoramas, in dem der weiße Turm des Rathauses in all seiner Eleganz hervorsticht.

En utilisant le fer et le verre pour la structure et la façade d'un immeuble destiné aux magasins Old England (1893), Paul Saintenoy fit œuvre de précurseur dans l'architecture Art Nouveau. La symétrie dominante est accentuée par le jeu des baies vitrées. L'Etat racheta l'ancien magasin de la rue Montagne de la Cour ainsi que le bâtiment néo-classique contigu, à l'angle de la place Royale. L'ensemble abrite depuis peu les remarquables collections du **musée des Instruments de musique**.

(Photo panoramique suivante)

Au sommet, un belvédère offre une vue panoramique de la place Royale à l'hôtel de ville. Aujourd'hui le café-restaurant du musée, il s'y accueillait autrefois le public mondain du salon de thé. À l'angle de la rue Villa-Hermosa, une tourelle se termine par une flèche de ferronnerie. L'on aperçoit, à gauche, la place du musée et le palais de Charles de Lorraine et, à droite à l'arrière-plan, la tour de l'hôtel de ville.

Met het gebruik van ijzer en glas voor de structuur en de voorgevel van een gebouw dat aan de Old England winkels toebehoort (1893), was Paul Saintenoy een voorloper in de Art Nouveau architectuur. De dominerende symmetrie wordt geaccentueerd door een stel schuifpuien. De staat kocht het oude winkelpand in de Hofbergstraat, evenals het aanpalende neoclassicistische gebouw op de hoek van het Koningsplein. Sinds kort bieden deze huizen onderdak aan de opmerkelijke collecties van het **museum van Muziekinstrumenten**.

(Volgende panoramische foto)

Bovenaan biedt een belvédère een panoramisch zicht, van het Koningsplein tot het stadhuis. Tegenwoordig is dit het café-restaurant van het museum, maar vroeger ontving men hier het mondaine publiek in het theesalon. Op de hoek van de Villa-Hermosastraat eindigt een torentje op een pijl in siersmeedwerk. Links ziet men het museumplein en het paleis van Karel van Lotharingen en rechts achteraan de toren van het stadhuis.

By his use in 1893 of glass and cast iron for the façade and structure of the building to house the "Old England" store, Paul Saintenoy was a precursor of Art Nouveau architecture. The dominant symmetry is accentuated by the placement of the great glass windows. The State bought the former store on Rue Montagne de la Cour as well as the adjoining neoclassical building on the corner of the Place Royale to house the remarkable collections of the recently opened **Museum of Musical Instruments**.

(Following panoramic photo)

At the top of the store a belvedere offers a panoramic view from the Place Royale to City Hall. Once a fashionable tea room it is now the café-restaurant of the museum. A turret on the corner of the Rue Villa-Hermosa ends in a cast iron spire. On the left is the Place du Musée and the palace of Charles of Lorraine and on the right in the background rises the spire of City Hall.

Durch die Verwendung von Eisen und Glas für die Struktur und Fassade eines für das Warenhaus Old England (1893) bestimmten Gebäudes schuf Paul Saintenoy ein Werk, das zum Wegbereiter in der Architektur des Art Nouveau wurde. Die dominante Symmetrie wird durch das Spiel der großen Glasfenster betont. Der Staat kaufte das ehemalige Geschäft der Rue Montagne de la Cour sowie das angrenzende neoklassizistische Gebäude an der Ecke der Place Royale. Der Komplex beherbergt seit kurzem die bemerkenswerten Sammlungen des **Musikinstrumentenmuseums**.

(Die folgenden Dreifachseiten)

Ganz oben bietet eine Aussichtsterrasse einen Rundblick von der Place Royale bis zum Rathaus. In dem heutigen Restaurant-Café des Museums fanden sich ehedem die mondänen Besucher des Teesalons ein. An der Ecke der Rue Villa-Hermosa schließt ein Türmchen mit einem schmiedeeisernen Pfeil ab. Links sind die Place du Musée und das Palais Karls v. Lothringen zu sehen, rechts erkennt man im Hintergrund den Rathausturm.

◁◁

Pour construire le **Palais des Beaux-Arts**, Victor Horta ne se heurta pas seulement aux irrégularités du terrain à flanc de coteau; l'exigence de ne pas masquer la perspective depuis la place des Palais lui imposa aussi de ne pas dépasser une certaine hauteur. Il lui fallut donc creuser pour obtenir le volume nécessaire à la grande salle Henri Le Bœuf, l'une des plus prestigieuses d'Europe, en particulier lors des finales du Concours international de Musique fondé par la reine Elisabeth.

Victor Horta had to contend not only with the irregularities of the sloping hillside terrain on which the **Palais des Beaux-Arts** was to be constructed but also with height limitations so as to not obstruct the perspective from the Place des Palais. It was necessary, therefore, to excavate deeply to obtain the desired dimensions for the great Henri Le Bœuf concert hall, one of the most prestigious in Europe, especially during the finals of the International Music Competition founded by Queen Elizabeth.

Toen hij de plannen van het **Paleis voor Schone Kunsten** ontwierp, stond Victor Horta voor twee problemen: de oneffenheden van het hellende bouwperceel en het verbod het uitzicht van op het Paleizenplein te benemen, hetgeen hem beperkingen oplegde in de hoogte. Bijgevolg waren grootscheepse uitgravingen vereist om voldoende ruimte te scheppen voor de grote Henry Le Bœufzaal, één der meest prestigieuze van Europa, waarin o.a. de finales van de Koningin Elisabethwedstrijden plaatshebben.

Bei der Erbauung des **Palasts der Schönen Künste** musste Victor Horta nicht nur den Unebenheiten des ansteigenden Geländes Rechnung tragen, er durfte auch die Aussicht vom Place des Palais aus nicht versperren, also praktisch nicht in die Höhe bauen. Der große Henry Le Bœuf Saal, einer der prachtvollsten Europas, in dem u.a. die Schlusskonzerte des Concours Reine Elisabeth stattfinden, wurde deshalb in einer riesigen, ausgebaggerten Baugrube errichtet.

En 1890, sur la pente douce qui descend vers le flanc droit de Notre-Dame du Sablon, naquit un gracieux jardin, le **Petit Sablon**. Le charme du site réside dans les quarante-huit colonnettes gothiques, chacune supportant la personnification d'une des corporations bruxelloises.

In 1890, a pretty garden was laid out on the gentle slope descending to the right side of Notre-Dame du Sablon, the **Petit Sablon**. The most charming feature is the 48 Gothic colonettes, each supporting a personification of one of the guilds of Brussels.

In 1890 werd er een bekoorlijke tuin aangelegd op de zachte helling aan de rechterkant van de Zavelkerk : de **Kleine Zavel**. De eigenlijke charme ervan komt van de achtenveertig gotische zuiltjes waarop telkens één van de oude Brusselse gilden door een personage wordt voorgesteld.

1890 entstand auf dem sanften Abhang rechts von der Kirche Notre-Dame du Sablon ein anmutiger Garten, der Platz des **Petit Sablon**. Er verdankt seinen eigentlichen Reiz den achtundvierzig gotischen Säulchen, auf deren Spitze jeweils ein Vertreter einer der vielen Zünfte Brüssels dargestellt ist.

Fondée par le Grand Serment des Arbalétriers, l'**église Notre-Dame des Victoires au Sablon** apparaît comme l'ultime fleuron du style gothique tardif à Bruxelles. De robustes contreforts contrebutent le chevet de l'église. Ils sont ornés de niches à statuettes, de gargouilles et de pinacles. La toute récente restauration met pleinement en valeur ce que l'on peut considérer comme les seuls éléments de style authentiquement gothique flamboyant de l'extérieur de l'église.

L'intérieur révèle l'évolution du gothique tertiaire pendant les cent années de la construction de l'église (1348-1435). La nef principale est séparée des nefs latérales par huit colonnes cylindriques et quatre gros piliers, tandis que le chœur est éclairé par de hautes fenêtres d'une seule venue.

De voor het Grooteedverbond der Kruisboogschutters gebouwde **O.-L.-Vrouwkerk van de Zavel** is als het ware de laatste bloesem van de laat-gotische stijl in Brussel. Robuste steunberen schragen de abside van de kerk. Ze zijn versierd met beeldjes in nissen, met spuiers en pinakels. Deze elementen, die men kan beschouwen als de enige in authentiek flamboyante gotische stijl aan de buitenkant van de kerk, komen dankzij de recente restauratie goed tot uiting.

Daar de bouw van de kerk een hele eeuw duurde (1348-1435), is het interieur een schoolvoorbeeld van de evolutie van de laatgotische stijl. Tussen het hoofdschip en de zijbeuken rijzen acht cilindervormige zuilen en vier stevige pilaren omhoog, terwijl het koor in licht baadt dankzij de hoge, rechtopgaande ramen.

Our Lady of the Sablon, the crowning jewel of late Gothic architecture in Brussels, was commissioned by the Solemn Order of Crossbow-men. Sturdy buttresses shore up the apses of the church. They are decorated with niches for statuettes, gargoyles and pinnacles. A recent restoration now shows to advantage what may be considered as the only true Flamboyant Gothic elements of the church's exterior.

The interior shows the evolution of late Gothic over the one hundred years it took to build the church (1348-1435). The nave is separated from the side aisles by eight cylindrical columns and four thick pillars. The choir is illuminated by high undivided windows.

Die von der Großen Armbrustschützenbruderschaft errichtete und der Muttergottes gewidmete **Kirche Notre-Dame du Sablon** ist die letzte Blüte der Spätgotik in Brüssel. Starke Strebepfeiler stützen die Apsis der Kirche. Sie werden von Nischen mit kleinen Statuen, Wasserspeiern und Fialen geschmückt. Die jüngste Restaurierung bringt diese Elemente als die einzigen Merkmale des echten spätgotischen Stils am Außenwerk der Kirche voll zur Geltung.

Das Innere der Kirche spiegelt die verschiedenen Entwicklungsphasen der Spätgotik wider, da die Errichtung ein ganzes Jahrhundert dauerte (1348-1435). Acht runde Säulen und vier wuchtige Pfeiler trennen das Hauptschiff von den Seitenschiffen. Das Chor badet im Sonnenlicht, das durch die hohen, durch nichts in ihrem Aufschwung gehemmten Fenster hereinströmt.

Au XVIᵉ siècle, les comtes d'Egmont possédaient un ensemble de bâtiments dans le quartier de la rue aux Laines, proche des fortifications de Bruxelles. Les Arenberg les acquirent au siècle suivant, les restaurèrent, agrandirent ou reconstruisirent, notamment après l'incendie de 1892. Le **Palais d'Egmont** ne cessa donc de se transformer jusqu'à l'aménagement en 1971 par l'État belge, qui l'avait acheté en 1964 pour y établir des salles de réceptions et les salons du Ministère des Affaires Etrangères.

Quatorze ans après l'incendie de 1892, la princesse de Croy eut l'idée de reconstituer dans le Palais d'Egmont l'«**escalier des Ambassadeurs**», que Le Vau avait conçu pour le château de Versailles et que Louis XV supprima en 1752. Les groupes en marbre (XVIIIᵉ siècle) sont inspirés de deux enlèvements célèbres : celui de Proserpine par Pluton et celui des Sabines par les Romains.

In de Wolstraat en vlak bij de toenmalige stadsomwalling bezaten de graven van Egmont in de 16de eeuw een heel gebouwencomplex, dat in de 17de eeuw te beurt viel aan de Arenbergs. Het geheel werd daarna gerestaureerd, vergroot en na de brand van 1892 weer opgebouwd. De verbouwingen namen pas een einde, nadat de Belgische Staat het **Egmontpaleis** in 1964 had overgenomen. In 1971 werden er de ontvangzalen en salons van het Ministerie voor Buitenlandse Zaken ingericht.

Veertien jaar na de brand van 1892 liet prinses de Croy de beroemde "**Trap der Gezanten**", die Le Vau voor het paleis van Versailles had ontworpen, maar die Lodewijk XV in 1752 had afgeschaft, in het Egmontpaleis heropbouwen. De marmeren beeldgroepen (18de eeuw) verwijzen naar bekende ontvoeringen : de roof van Persephone door Hades en de Sabijnse maagdenroof.

In the 16th century the Counts of Egmont possessed an ensemble of buildings in the Rue des Laines quarter, near the fortifications. In the following century they were acquired by the Arenberg family who restored or rebuilt them particularly after the fire of 1892. Thus the **Egmont Palace** was constantly being remodelled until the Belgian state, which bought it in 1964 to serve for receptions and meetings organized by the Ministry of Foreign Affairs, finished the work in 1971.

Fourteen years after the fire of 1892 the Princess de Croy decided to reconstruct in the Egmont Palace the "**Ambassadors Staircase**" that Le Vau had designed for Versailles, demolished by Louis XV in 1752. The 18th century marble groups are inspired by two celebrated abductions : that of Proserpine by Pluto and that of the Sabine women by the Romans.

In der Nähe der Rue aux Laines und der Stadtmauer besaßen die Grafen von Egmont im 16. Jh. Baulichkeiten, die im 17. Jh. an die von Arenberg übergingen, danach restauriert und vergrößert und nach dem Brand von 1892 schließlich wieder aufgebaut wurden. Im **Egmontpalais**, das seit 1964 dem belgischen Staat gehört, wurden 1971 Empfangssäle und andere Empfangsräume für das dort angesiedelte Außenministerium eingerichtet.

Vierzehn Jahre nach dem Brand von 1892 beschloss die Prinzessin de Croy, im Egmontpalais die "**Treppe der Gesandten**", die Le Vau für Versailles entworfen, Ludwig XV. jedoch 1752 abgeschafft hatte, wieder entstehen zu lassen. Die Marmorgruppen (18. Jh.) haben beide eine berühmte Entführungsszene zum Thema: die Proserpinas durch Pluto und den Raub der Sabinerinnen.

(Ci-dessus)

Place Royale, la statue en pied de Charles de Lorraine qui avait été fondue pendant l'occupation française fut remplacée en 1848 par la statue équestre de **Godefroi de Bouillon**. Le héros incontesté de la première Croisade avait été élu roi de Jérusalem par les barons, après la prise de cette ville le 22 juillet 1099, mais il se contenta du titre d'avoué du Saint-Sépulcre. À l'autre bout de la rue de la Régence, le titanesque palais de Justice est momentanément revêtu d'échafaudages.

(Page de droite)

En 1878 fut solennellement inaugurée la **grande synagogue** de la rue de la Régence, construite en style romano-byzantin. Dans l'abside richement polychromée et dorée, sur une estrade – le *bimah* – précédée des traditionnels chandeliers à sept branches, la monumentale Arche d'Alliance renferme les rouleaux de la torah, la loi de Moïse.

(Hierboven)

Op het Koningsplein stond een standbeeld van Karel van Lorreinen dat tijdens de Frans bezetting werd omgesmolten. In 1848 werd het vervangen door een ruiterstandbeeld van **Godfried van Bouillon**, wiens leiderschap tijdens de eerste kruistocht onbetwist is. De baronnen hadden hem tot koning van Jeruzalem verkozen na de val van die stad op 22 juli 1099, maar Godfried weigerde alle eretitels behalve die van beschermheer van het Heilig Graf. Aan het andere eind van de Regentschapsstraat rijst het reusachtige Justitiepaleis op, dat in de steigers stond toen onze foto werd genomen.

(Rechterbladzijde)

In 1878 werd de **grote synagoge** van de Regenschapstraat, in romaans-byzantijnse stijl, plechtig ingehuldigd. In de rijkelijk vergulde en veelkleurige abside, op een verhoging – de bimah – omsluit de monumentale Ark des Verbonds de rollen van de thora, de wet van Mozes, voorafgegaan door de traditionele zevenarmige kandelaars.

(Above)

The full-length statue of Charles of Lorraine which stood in the Place Royale until it was melted down under the French occupation was replaced in 1848 by the equestrian statue of **Godfrey of Bouillon**. The peerless hero of the First Crusade was elected King of Jerusalem by the barons after the city fell to the Crusaders on July 22, 1099 but he declined this title and took that of Advocate, or Protector, of the Holy Sepulchre. At the other end of Rue de la Régence the titanic Law Courts are temporily covered with scaffolding.

(Page right)

The **great synagogue**, built in a Romanesque-Byzantine style on the Rue de la Régence, was officially opened in 1878. On the dais – the *bimah* – in the richly polychromed and gilded apse is the monumental Ark of the Covenant containing the Torah, the Mosaic Law, preceded by the traditional menorahs.

(Oben)

Nachdem die französische Besatzung das auf dem Place Royale errichtete Standbild Karls von Lothringen eingeschmolzen hatte, wurde es 1848 durch ein Reiterstandbild von **Gottfried von Bouillon** ersetzt, dessen Führerschaft während des ersten Kreuzzugs unbestritten ist. Nachdem Jerusalem am 22. Juli 1099 gefallen war, wollten ihn die Barone zum König des Heiligen Landes ausrufen, doch aus Bescheidenheit ließ er sich nur zum Schirmherrn des Hl. Grabes ernennen. Am andere Ende der Rue de la Régence erhebt sich der gigantische Justizplalast.

(Rechte Seite)

Im Jahre 1878 wurde die im romanisch-byzantinischen Stil erbaute **große Synagoge** in der Rue de la Régence feierlich eingeweiht. In der monumentalen Bundeslade, die auf einem Podest – dem bimah – in der äußerst polychromen und vergoldeten Apsis steht und vor der sich die traditionellen siebenarmigen Leuchter befinden, werden die Rollen der Thora, dem mosaischen Gesetz, aufbewahrt.

◁△

Lourdement posé sur le *Galgenberg* (Montagne des Potences), où l'anatomiste André Vésale venait nuitamment dérober des cadavres de suppliciés, le **Palais de Justice** (1866-1883) couvre une superficie de vingt-six mille mètres carrés. Né de l'imagination fébrile de l'architecte Poelaert, il conjugue tous les styles : gréco-romain, babylonien, assyrien et même égyptien. Son dôme s'élève à cent dix-huit mètres de hauteur.

Zwaar drukkend op de *Galgenberg*, waar de ontleedkundige Andreas Vesalius 's nachts de lijken van de ter dood gebrachten kwam stelen, beslaat het **Justitiepaleis** (1866-1883) een oppervlakte van 26.000 vierkante meter. Het is een mengsel van alle stijlen: Grieks-Romeinse, Babylonische, Assyrische en zelfs Egyptische ontstaan uit het koortsige brein van architect Poelaert. De koepel is 118 meter hoog.

Dominating the **Galgenberg** (Gallow's Hill), where the anatomist Vesalius used to come at night to steal the bodies of executed criminals, the **Law Courts** (1866-1883) cover an area of over 26,000 square meters. Due to the feverish imagination of the architect Poelaert, it combines many styles : Greco-Roman, Babylonian, Assyrian, and even Egyptian. The dome rises to over 118 meters.

Wie ein Ungetüm steht der **Justizpalast** (1866-1883) auf dem *Galgenberg*, auf dem der Anatom A. Vesalius einst Leichen von Hingerichteten entwendet hatte. Das 26.000 qm große Gebäude wurde vom Architekten und Phantasten Poelaert entworfen, der hier alle Baustile, griechisch-römische, babylonische, assyrische und ägyptische, miteinander verquickte. Die Kuppel ist 118 m hoch.

▷▷

Située dans le haut de la ville, sur le boulevard de la *petite ceinture* entre la porte de Hal et la porte de Namur, la **place Louise** porte le nom de la fille aînée de Léopold II, tout comme l'avenue qui la relie au Bois de la Cambre. La proximité de plusieurs hôtels et galeries, la variété des commerces de luxe font du quartier l'un des plus huppés de Bruxelles.

Het in de bovenstad gelegen **Louizaplein**, op de Kleine Ring tussen de Hallepoort en de Naamsepoort, heeft zijn naam te danken aan de oudste dochter van Leopold II, net zoals de laan die van het plein naar het Ter Kamerenbos loopt. Met zijn hotels, galerijen en zijn waaier van luxewinkels is het één van de elegantste wijken van de stad.

Situated in the upper town on the *petite ceinture* or inner ring between the Porte de Namur and the Porte de Hal, **Place Louise** bears the name of the eldest daughter of Leopold II, as does the avenue linking it to the entrance of the La Cambre woods. Set in a quarter of hotels, galeries and luxurious shops, it is one of the most exclusive areas of Brussels.

Place Louise befindet sich in der Oberstadt, und zwar auf dem "Kleinen Ring" zwischen Porte de Hal und Porte de Namur. Wie die Straße, die vom Platz bis zum Bois de la Cambre führt, trägt er den Namen der ältesten Tochter Leopolds II. Die umliegenden Hotels, die Galerien und die vielen, oft sehr unterschiedlichen Luxusgeschäfte machen diesen Stadtteil zum vornehmsten Brüssels.

La **Porte de Hal** est le seul vestige de la deuxième enceinte de Bruxelles (XIVe siècle). Elle échappa à la destruction des portes ordonnée en 1786, puis au démantèlement complet des remparts au cours du premier tiers du XIXe siècle. Elle servit successivement de grenier à blé, de cachot militaire, d'église luthérienne et de prison avant d'être affectée en dépôt d'archives, et enfin en musée d'Armes et d'Antiquité jusqu'à la fin du XXe siècle. Le bâtiment fut considérablement transformé en 1868 par l'architecte Henri Beyaert.

(Ci-dessus)
La tour d'escalier est née de l'imagination fertile de Beyaert. De style néo-gothique, l'escalier à vis est garni de garde-corps en ferronnerie et les chapiteaux portent des statuettes en bronze.

(Photo panoramique précédente)

De **Hallepoort** is het enige resterende spoor van de tweede omwalling van Brussel (14de eeuw). Ze ontsnapte eerst aan de in 1786 opgelegde vernietiging van de poorten, daarna aan de complete ontmanteling van de omwallingen tijdens de eerste 30 jaren van de 19de eeuw. Ze deed achtereenvolgens dienst als tarwezolder, militaire gevangenis, lutheraanse kerk en burgergevangenis, tot ze een opslagplaats voor archieven werd, en tenslotte museum voor Wapens en Oudheidkunde tot aan het einde van de 20ste eeuw. Het gebouw werd in 1868 aanzienlijk getransformeerd door architect Henri Beyaert.

(Hierboven)
De traphal is ontsproten aan de vruchtbare verbeelding van Beyaert. De draaitrap, in neo-gotische stijl, is versierd met leuningen in siersmeedwerk en de kapitelen dragen bronzen standbeelden.

(Vorige panoramische foto)
Zuilen verdelen de grote wapenzaal, die ongeschonden uit de restauratie van de 19de eeuw kwam en momenteel leeg is. De zuilen dragen geen kapitelen en ondersteunen direct de gewelfribben. De grote renaissanceschouw komt uit het voormalige hotel van Cortenbach in Mechelen.

Des colonnes divisent la vaste salle d'armes, sortie indemne de la restauration du XIXe siècle et actuellement vide. Dépourvues de chapiteaux, elles soutiennent directement les arcs doubleaux. La grande cheminée Renaissance provient de l'ancien hôtel de Cortenbach à Malines.

The **Porte de Hal** is the only vestige of the 14th century second set of Brussels' walls that survives. It escaped the destruction of the gates decreed in 1798 and then the complete demolition of the walls in the first third of the 19th century. It served successively for grain storage, as a military prison, a Lutheran church and a jail before being converted into an archives deposit and finally, until the end of the 20th century into an Arms and Antiquities museum. The building was greatly modified by the architect Henri Beyaert.

(Above)
The staircase tower was conceived in the fertile imagination of Beyaert. The spiral Gothic Revival staircase is embellished with decorative ironwork and the capitals support bronze statuettes.

(Preceding panoramic photo)
Columns divide the huge armoury, untouched by the 19th century restoration and now unfurnished. The columns have no capitals and support directly the transverse ribs. The great Renaissance fireplace comes from the former Cortenbach mansion in Mechelen.

Die **Porte de Hal** ist das einzige erhalten gebliebene Zeugnis der zweiten Stadtmauer von Brüssel (14. Jd.). Sie entging dem 1786 angeordneten Abriss der Tore und später dann dem vollständigen Schleifen der Befestigungsanlagen im Laufe des ersten Drittels des 19. Jahrhunderts. Das Torgebäude diente nacheinander als Getreidespeicher, Militärverlies, Lutheranerkirche und Gefängnis, bevor es als Lagerungsort für Archive genutzt wurde und schließlich bis Ende des 20. Jahrhunderts das Waffen- und Antikemuseum beherbergte. Das Tor wurde im Jahre 1868 von Architekt Henri Beyaert erheblich umgestaltet.

(Darüber)
Der Treppenturm entstammt der reichen Phantasie von Beyaert. Im neugotischem Stil erbaut, wird die Wendeltreppe von schmiedeeisernen Leibwächtern geschmückt, und die Kapitelle tragen kleine Bronzestatuen.

(Vorherige Dreifachseite)
Säulen unterteilen den geräumigen Waffensaal, der von der Restaurierung im 19. Jahrhundert unberührt geblieben ist und derzeit leer steht. Ohne Kapitelle stützen die Säulen direkt die Gurtbögen. Der große Renaissance-Kamin stammt aus dem ehemaligen Herrenhaus von Cortenbach in Mecheln.

Vu du sommet de la Porte de Hal, le panorama du **boulevard du Midi** ne révèle plus rien de l'ancien quartier des tisserands et des foulons, ni de la léproserie de Saint-Pierre. Au loin se dresse la moderne tour du Midi.

Vanaf de top van de Hallepoort verraadt het panorama van de **Zuidlaan** niets meer van de voormalige wevers- en volderswijk, noch van het leprozenhuis van Sint-Pieters. In de verte staat de moderne Zuidertoren.

The panorama of the **Boulevard du Midi** seen from the top of the Porte de Hal displays what was once the weavers and fullers district where the leprosarium of Saint Pierre stood. In the distance is the modern Midi tower.

Im architektonischen Bild des **Boulevard du Midi**, wie es sich von der Porte de Hal herab darbietet, finden sich keinerlei Spuren mehr von dem ehemaligen Viertel der Weber und Walkmühlen oder dem Lepraheim des Heiligen Petrus. In der Ferne erhebt sich der moderne Südturm (Tour du Midi).

Au cœur du quartier des Marolles, la **rue Haute** relie la Porte de Hal à la place de la Chapelle. Elle est bordée de maisons de différents styles, certaines très modestes, les autres plus ouvragées, datant des XVIᵉ et XVIIᵉ siècles. Pierre Bruegel l'Ancien a probablement vécu dans l'une d'elles; elle existe encore au numéro 132. Bien que demeuré populaire et populeux, le quartier s'est transformé grâce à la concentration de commerces d'antiquités qui attirent désormais une clientèle dite bon chic bon genre.

Rue Haute in the heart of the Marolles district links the Porte de Hal to the Place de la Chapelle. It is lined with houses in many different styles, some quite modest, others more elaborate of the 16th and 17th centuries. Peter Breughel the Elder likely lived in one of them, at number 132. Though still mainly populated by the working class the district has been changed by the many antique shops which now attract the wealthy carriage trade.

In het hart van de Marollenwijk verbindt de **Hoogstraat** de Hallepoort met de Kapellemarkt. In de straat staan huizen in verschillende stijlen, sommige erg bescheiden, andere meer verfijnd, daterend uit de 16de en de 17de eeuw. Pieter Brueghel de Oudere heeft waarschijnlijk in één van deze huizen gewoond; het huis is nog te vinden op het nummer 132. Hoewel deze wijk populair en dichtbevolkt is gebleven, onderging hij toch een gedaanteverwisseling dankzij de concentratie van antiekzaken die een 'bon chic bon genre' klienteel aantrekken.

Im Herzen des Marollenviertels verbindet die **Rue Haute** die Porte de Hal mit der Place de la Chapelle. Sie wird von Häusern aus dem 16. und 17. Jh. in verschiedenen Baustilen gesäumt, von denen einige sehr einfach, andere etwas kunstvoller gebaut sind. Pieter Brueghel d. Ä. lebte sehr wahrscheinlich in einem von ihnen, nämlich im Haus Nr. 132, das erhalten geblieben ist. Obgleich das Viertel volkstümlich und dichtbewohnt geblieben ist, hat es sich doch durch die Konzentration von Antiquitätenläden verändert, die nun die sog. Schickimicki-Kundschaft anziehen.

Quand Pierre Bruegel fut inhumé en 1569 dans l'**église Notre-Dame de la Chapelle**, celle-ci existait déjà depuis trois siècles et demi. Le premier édifice était purement roman (vers 1134). La partie la plus ancienne de l'église actuelle se situe aux piliers occidentaux de la croisée (1210); leur section cruciforme, à double ressaut, donne l'illusion du roman mais l'arc brisé qui les unit témoigne de la transition gothique. Appartiennent au XIIIᵉ siècle aussi, le croisillon nord, la croisée du transept, la tour centrale et le chœur. La nef lumineuse et élancée date du XVᵉ siècle, tandis que la tour posée sur piliers resta inachevée en 1508. Elle ne reçut son couronnement bulbeux qu'après le bombardement de Bruxelles en 1695.

Une inscription indique l'emplacement exact de la sépulture de Pierre Bruegel l'Ancien.

(Page 68)

Le chœur du XIIIᵉ siècle a, depuis peu, retrouvé l'éclat de son abondante polychromie néo-gothique. Pour dessiner les vitraux, Charles-Albert – le décorateur du château de Gaasbeek – s'est souvenu de ceux de Bourges, en France. Ils représentent les évangélistes, quatre prophètes et des scènes de la vie du Christ.

De **Kapellekerk** was reeds driehonderd vijftig jaar oud toen Pieter Bruegel er in 1569 werd begraven. Oorspronkelijk (1134) was het een Romaans gebouw. Het oudste gedeelte van de huidige kerk zijn de westelijke pilaren van de kruisbeuk (1210). De kruisvormige pilaren met dubbele verbreding doen natuurlijk aan de Romaanse bouwkunst denken, maar de spitsboog die ze met elkaar verbindt, wijst op gotische invloed. De noordelijke kruisbeuk, de viering en de centrale toren dateren uit de 13de eeuw, evenals het kunstig afgewerkte koor. De mooi verlichte, slanke middenbeuk werd in de 15de eeuw voltooid, terwijl aan de sinds 1508 onafgewerkte toren pas na het bombardement van 1695 een ietwat gedrongen torenspits werd toegevoegd.

Een inscriptie in de kerk wijst de plaats aan waar Pieter Bruegel de Oude begraven werd.

(Bladzijde 68)

Het 13de-eeuwse koor heeft sinds kort de luister van zijn overvloedige neo-gotische polychromie teruggevonden. Voor het ontwerp van de glasramen liet Charles-Albert – de decorateur van het kasteel van Gaasbeek – zich inspireren door die in Bourges, in Frankrijk. Ze beelden de evangelisten af, vier profeten en scènes uit het leven van Christus.

When Peter Bruegel was buried in the **Church of Notre-Dame de la Chapelle**, in 1569, the building was already three and a half centuries old. The first church, begun around 1134, was in pure Romanesque style, but the west pillars of the transept crossing which date from 1210 are the oldest elements of the present church. These cruciform pillars with double projections look Romanesque but the Gothic arch between them indicates the transitional Gothic period. The north arm of the transept, the crossing , and the central tower are all 13th century, as is the choir. The soaring, luminous nave dates from the 15th century. The tower, rising on pillars, was left unfinished in 1508. The onion dome was added after the bombardment of Brussels in 1695.

An inscription marks the exact spot where Peter Bruegel the Elder lies.

(Following page)

The 13th century choir has recently had its Gothic revival polychrome décor restored. Charles-Albert, decorator of Gaasbeek castle, drew inspiration from Bourges in France for the stained glass windows, depicting the Evangelists, four prophets and scenes from the life of Christ.

Als Pieter Bruegel 1569 in der **Kirche Notre-Dame de la Chapelle** beigesetzt wurde, bestand diese schon seit dreieinhalb Jahrhunderten. Die ursprüngliche Kirche (1134) war in rein romanischem Stil gebaut. Der älteste Teil der heutigen Kirche sind die westlichen Pfeiler in der Nähe der Vierung (1210). Ihr kreuzförmiger Schnitt mit doppeltem Vorsprung gleicht dem romanischer Bauformen, doch die Bögen, die sie oben verbinden, weisen auf den Übergang zur Gotik. Der nördliche Teil des Querschiffes, das Quadrat der Vierung, der Mittelturm und das Chor entstanden ebenfalls im 13. Jh. Das helle, schlanke Hauptschiff wurde im 15. Jh. gebaut, während der seit 1508 unvollendete Turm erst nach der Beschießung von 1695 seine zwiebelförmige Spitze erhielt.

Eine Inschrift in der Kirche gibt die Stelle an, an der Pieter Bruegel der Ältere begraben liegt.

(Folgende Seite)

Der Chor aus dem 13. Jahrhundert erhielt jüngst den Glanz seiner reichen neugotischen Polychromie zurück. Bei der Gestaltung der Glasfenster ließ sich Charles-Albert, der Dekorationsmaler des Schlosses von Gaasbeek, von den Kirchenfenstern von Bourges in Frankreich inspirieren. Sie stellen die Evangelisten, vier Propheten und Szenen aus dem Leben Jesu dar.

Située boulevard de l'Empereur non loin de l'église de la Chapelle, la **tour Anneessens** s'appelait jadis *Pijntoren* parce qu'on y soumettait les accusés à la torture. Bien que mal environnée, elle confirme qu'en cet endroit les remparts formaient un coude qui imposait la construction d'un solide ouvrage de deux étages.

De zg. **Anneessenstoren** in de Keizerslaan in de buurt van de Kapellekerk werd vroeger Pijntoren genoemd, omdat de beschuldigden er werden gefolterd. Niettegenstaande de weinig gunstige omgeving ziet men duidelijk dat de omwalling hier een haakse bocht maakte, zodat een versterkingswerk met twee verdiepingen noodzakelijk was.

On the Boulevard de l'Empereur, not far from the Church de la Chapelle, the so-called **Anneessens tower** was called formerly the "Pyntoren", or tower of pain, because it was there that the accused were tortured. Although now hemmed in, it shows that at this point the ramparts made a sharp bend, requiring a sturdy, two-storey edifice.

Am Boulevard de l'Empereur, in der Nähe der Kapellenkirche steht der sog. **Anneessens Turm**, der früher Peinturm hieß, weil die Beschuldigten dort gefoltert wurden. Trotz der unangebrachten Umgebung kann man feststellen, dass der hier abgewinkelte Schutzwall die Errichtung eines robusten, zweistöckigen Baus erforderlich machte.

△▷

C'est au cours de la première moitié du XIIIᵉ siècle qu'une enceinte donna à Bruxelles un caractère véritablement urbain. Le tracé de ses quatre kilomètres de murailles était jalonné de sept portes et d'une quarantaine de tours défensives. Cette première enceinte, haute de dix mètres, tirait profit des étangs existants sur le versant oriental de la vallée de la Senne. Quelques vestiges subsistent de ce puissant rempart de grès, notamment la muraille crénelée qui jouxte la **tour de Villers**. On peut la découvrir dans la cour du Sint-Jorisinstituut au 16 rue des Alexiens et son avers rue de Villers.

Brussel werd pas echt een stad, toen tussen 1200 en 1250 de eerste, ongeveer 4 km lange stadsomwalling met zeven poorten en zowat veertig vestingtorens werd gebouwd. Ze was 10 m hoog en vooral aan de oostkant van de Zennevallei was ze van sloten en bijkomende vijvers voorzien. Overblijfsels van deze zandstenen omwalling, o.a. de gekanteelde muur naast de **Villerstoren** zijn nog van op het speelplein van het St.-Jorisinstituut, Cellebroersstraat 16, te zien; de veldkant van de muur ligt langs de Villersstraat.

During the first half of the 13th century walls gave Brussels a true urban character. The four kilometers of walls were studded with seven gates and forty-odd defensive towers. This first ten-meter high wall took advantage of the existing ponds on the east slope of the Senne valley. A few vestiges of those powerful sandstone ramparts still exist, in particular the crenellated wall abutting on the **Villers tower**. The remains can be seen in the courtyard of the Sint-Jorisinstituut at 16 Rue des Alexiens which also backs on Rue de Villers.

Die Errichtung der ersten Stadtmauer in der ersten Hälfte des 13. Jh. machte Brüssel erst zu einer vollwertigen Stadt. Die 4 km lange Mauer hatte sieben Tore und war mit etwa vierzig Verteidigungstürmen versehen. Sie war 10 m hoch; Sümpfe die Senne entlang verstärkten sie vor allem an der Ostseite. Von diesem wuchtigen Schutzwall aus Sandstein sind einige Reste übriggeblieben, z.B. die ausgezackte Mauer am **Villers Turm**, deren Stadtseite man vom Schulplatz des St.-Jorinsinstituut (Rue des Alexiens, 16) und deren Landseite man von der Rue de Villers aus sehen kann.

△

La première enceinte du XIIIᵉ siècle contournait ce qui était alors l'église Sainte-Gudule. Comme c'était l'usage, des bâtisses y étaient adossées. La **maison du doyen de la cathédrale**, rue du Bois Sauvage face au chevet du sanctuaire, date de 1610. Sa façade enjolivée d'une tourelle ronde donne sur une petite cour. Quelques vestiges de l'enceinte existent encore dans le jardin.

De eerste omwalling van de 13de eeuw omringde wat toen de Sint-Goedelekerk was. Zoals destijds gebruikelijk, waren kleinere gebouwtjes opgetrokken tegen de muren. De **dekenij van de kathedraal**, in de Wildewoudstraat tegenover de abside, dateert van 1610. De hoofdgevel is opgesmukt met een rond torentje en geeft uit op een kleine binnenplaats. In de tuin zijn nog enkele overblijfselen te vinden van de omwalling.

The first city walls of the 13th century went around what was then the church of Saint Gudule. As was then common, houses were built against it. The **house of the Dean of the cathedral** on Rue du Bois Sauvage facing the apse of the cathedral dates from 1610. The façade enlivened by a round turret gives on a little courtyard. A few vestiges of the wall still exist in the garden.

Die erste Umfassungsmauer aus dem 13. Jahrhundert umgab die damalige St.-Gudula Kirche. Wie es Brauch war, lehnten sich Gebäude daran an. Das **Haus des Dekans der Kathedrale** in der Rue du Bois Sauvage gegenüber der Apsis des Altarraums stammt aus dem Jahre 1610. Seine mit einem runden Türmchen verzierte Fassade weist auf einen kleinen Hof. Im Garten finden sich noch einige Überreste der Stadtmauer.

▷

La construction de la **cathédrale Saint-Michel** commença sous le règne du duc de Brabant Henri Iᵉʳ. Après une interruption momentanée, les travaux reprirent vers 1273 dans le style gothique plus avancé. Au cours des XIVᵉ et XVᵉ siècles, la nef de l'ancienne église romane disparut au profit d'une nef de style gothique brabançon. La tour sud fut terminée vers 1451 et la tour nord quelques années plus tard.

Onder hertog Hendrik I werd er een aanvang gemaakt met het bouwen van de **St. Michielskathedraal**. Na een kortstondige onderbreking begon rond 1273 de tweede bouwfase in een reeds rijpere gotische stijl. In de loop van de 14de en de 15de eeuw werd het Romaanse kerkschip door Brabants-gotische beuken vervangen. De zuidertoren had zijn huidige vorm al rond 1451, de noordertoren enkele jaren daarna.

Construction of **St. Michael's Cathedral** began under the reign of Henry I, Duke of Brabant. After a short interlude work began anew around 1273 in a more developed Gothic style. During the 14th and 15th centuries the nave of the old Romanesque church was rebuilt in the Brabantine Gothic style. The south tower was finished around 1451 and the north tower a few years later.

Der Bau der **St. Michaelskathedrale** wurde unter der Regierung des Herzogs von Brabant Heinrich I. in Angriff genommen. Nach einer kurzen Unterbrechung baute man 1273 im inzwischen zur Blüte gelangten gotischen Stil weiter. Im 14. und 15. Jh. wurde das romanische Schiff durch ein neues in brabantisch-gotischem Stil ersetzt. Der Bau des südlichen Turms wurde 1451, der des nördlichen etwas später abgeschlossen.

△ Depuis peu, l'intérieur de la **cathédrale Saint-Michel** a retrouvé toute sa splendeur d'antan. À partir du transept, trois phases du style gothique s'offrent au regard. Il est primaire (XIII siècle) dans le chœur *(à droite)*. À chacune des trois travées droites, les lourdes colonnes cylindriques s'achèvent par des chapiteaux à feuilles enroulées semblables à ceux de la nef. Le dessin du triforium, la galerie sous les fenêtres, adapte en plus robuste le modèle français : par travée, trois arcs aigus encadrent chacun deux arcs plus petits. Le déambulatoire du chœur appartient au gothique de transition. Il fut achevé sous l'impulsion personnelle du duc de Brabant Jean Ier.

Au nord, la grande chapelle du Saint Sacrement *(à gauche)* aux vitraux de Bernard van Orley remplace quatre chapelle rayonnantes détruites en 1533. Elle est représentative du gothique à l'époque de Charles Quint.

Sinds kort heeft het interieur van de **Sint-Michielskathedraal** haar luister van weleer teruggevonden. Vanaf het dwarsschip ontvouwen zich drie fasen van de gotische stijl. De eerste fase (13de eeuw) vindt men in het koor *(rechts)*. Aan elk van de drie rechte traveeën eindigen zware ronde zuilen in kapitelen met opgerolde bladeren zoals die in de hoofdbeuk. Het ontwerp van het triforium, de galerij onder de ramen, volgt het Franse model: per travee omkaderen drie spitsbogen elk twee kleinere bogen. De kooromgang behoort tot de transitie-gotiek. Hij werd afgewerkt onder de persoonlijke impuls van de Hertog van Brabant, Jan I.

In het noorden vervangt de grote kapel van het Heilige Sacrament *(links)* met glasramen van Barend van Orley de vier schitterende kapellen die in 1533 werden vernietigd. Deze kapel is representatief voor de gotische stijl ten tijde van Karel de Vijfde.

The interior of **Saint Michael's cathedral** has been recently restored to its original splendour. From the transept three different phases of the Gothic style can be seen. The choir _(right)_ is early Gothic of the 13th century. In each of the three right bays massive cylindrical columns end in capitals of rolled up leaves like those of the nave. The design of the triforium, the gallery under the windows, is a sturdier adaptation of the French model. In each bay three pointed arches frame two smaller ones. The ambulatory of the choir belongs to transitional Gothic. Jean I, Duke of Brabant personally influenced its completion.

To the north the large chapel of the Holy Sacrament _(left)_ with stained glass windows by Bernard van Orley replaced four rayonnant chapels destroyed in 1533. It is typical of the gothic style during the period of Charles the Fifth.

Seit kurzem hat das Innere der **St.-Michaelskathedrale** zu seiner ganzen früheren Herrlichkeit zurückgefunden. Vom Querschiff aus bieten sich dem Betrachter drei Phasen der Gotik dar. Frühgotik (13. Jd.) im Chorraum _(rechts)_. An jedem der drei geraden Gewölbefelder enden die schweren zylindrischen Säulen in Kapitellen mit eingerollten Blättern gleich denen im Kirchenschiff. Bei der Gestaltung des Triforiums, des Laufgangs unter den Fenstern, wurde das französische Modell in robusterer Ausführung übernommen: Je Gewölbefeld rahmen drei Spitzbögen jeweils zwei kleinere Bögen ein. Der Chorumgang gehört einer Übergangsform der Gotik an. Er wurde unter dem persönlichen Auftrag des Herzogs von Brabant, Johann I., fertiggestellt.

Im Norden ersetzt die große Hl. Sakraments-Kapelle _(links)_ mit Fenstern von Barend van Orley vier Kapellenkränze, die im Jahre 1533 zerstört worden waren. Sie repräsentiert die Gotik zur Zeit Karls des Fünften.

De saint augustin en bing sermon.
Comme on ne peut nettoier
ne curer les pechies par ſu
ne mais ce fait on bien
par aumoſne la ſoit ce q
line ſoit bonne. Touteſfoi
ce mieulx vault aumoſne. Et ſe on peut
faire tous les deux il est bon et est dou
ble bien. Mais ſe on ne les peut faire
tous deux mieulx vault donner aumoſne.

(Ci-dessus)

Marguerite d'York, la troisième épouse de Charles le Téméraire, fit exécuter cette **miniature** entre 1468 et 1477. Le peintre de l'école bruxelloise de Jean Dreux l'a représentée agenouillé devant sainte Marguerite et entourée des quatre Docteurs de l'Eglise. À l'arrière-plan, de gauche à droite : l'église inachevée de Notre-Dame du Sablon, la collégiale des Saints-Michel-et-Gudule et la silhouette de l'ancien beffroi de l'église Saint-Nicolas (Bibliothèque Royale Albert Iᵉʳ).

(À droite)

Dans la chapelle du Saint-Sacrement, le vitrail peint en 1540, œuvre de Bernard van Orley, représente François Iᵉʳ, roi de France, et la reine Eléonore. Les souverains sont agenouillés, leurs saints patrons se tiennent debout.

(Hierboven)

Margareta van York, de derde echtgenote van Karel de Stoute, gaf tussen 1468 en 1477 opdracht tot het tekenen en schilderen van deze **miniatuur**. Een kunstenaar van de Brusselse school van Jean Dreux, tekende haar neergeknield voor de heilige Margareta en omgeven door vier kerkleraren. Op de achtergrond zien we van links naar rechts de nog onvoltooide O.-L.-Vrouwkerk van de Zavel, de St.-Michiels- en St.-Goedelekerk en de omtrekken van het oude belfort van de St.-Niklaaskerk (Koninklijke Bibliotheek Albert I).

(Rechterbladzijde)

In de kapel van het Heilige Sacrament hangt een gebrandschilderd glasraam uit 1540 van de hand van Barend van Orley. Het is de afbeelding van Frans I, koning van Frankrijk, en koningin Eleonore, knielend naast hun beschermheiligen.

(Above)

Margaret of York, the third wife of Charles the Bold, commissionned this **miniature** painted by an artist of the Brussels school of Jean Dreux between 1468-1477. She is shown kneeling in front of St. Margaret, with the four Fathers of the Church. In the background, from left to right, are the unfinished church of Our Lady of the Sablon, the collegiate church of Saints Michael and Gudule, and the silhouette of the old belfry of St. Nicholas (Albert I Royal Library).

(Page right)

In the chapel of the Holy Sacrament the window painted in 1540 by Bernard van Orley depicts Francois I, King of France and his queen, Eleanor kneeling while their patron saints stand by them.

(Oben)

Margaretha von York, die dritte Gemahlin Karls des Kühnen, ließ diese **Miniatur** zwischen 1468 und 1477 anfertigen. Ein Maler der Brüsseler Schule, Jean Dreux, stellte die vor der heiligen Margaretha kniende Fürstin dar, umgeben von vier Kirchenlehrern. Im Hintergrund gewahrt man von rechts nach links die noch unvollendete Kirche Notre-Dame du Sablon, die St.-Michaelskathedrale (damals noch eine Stiftskirche) und den Umriss des Bergfrieds der St.-Nikolauskirche (Königliche Bibliothek Albert I.).

(Rechte Seite)

Das bunte Kirchenfenster in der Hl. Sakraments-Kapelle wurde 1540 von Barend van Orley geschaffen. Die zwei knienden Gestalten sind König Franz I. von Frankreich und Königin Eleonore, die stehenden ihre heiligen Schutzpatrone.

Désormais bordé par la Bibliothèque royale Albert Ier et le Palais des Congrès, le Mont des Arts amorce le périmètre de la **ville basse**. Celui-ci coïncide jusqu'au Carrefour de l'Europe avec la rue de la Madeleine *(à l'avant-plan)*, ainsi dénommée depuis le XVIIe siècle mais dont le tracé date du tout début du développement urbain.

À l'arrière-plan, juché à l'extrémité de la ville haute, le palais de Justice *(à gauche)* domine une partie du panorama malgré la présence incongrue de deux tours dont l'une semble vouloir écraser le clocher de l'église de la Chapelle, à la périphérie du quartier des Marolles.

Fort heureusement, autour de l'hôtel de ville et de la Grand-Place *(à droite)*, le tissu urbain est demeuré tel que l'organisa le Magistrat de Bruxelles après le bombardement de 1695.

Dans le lointain s'étendent les faubourgs qui ont définitivement perdu l'aspect rustique qu'ils avaient au siècle dernier.

Aucun fleuve ne traverse la ville, ce qui surprit l'écrivain français Gérard de Nerval. «Qu'est-ce qu'une capitale où l'on n'a pas la faculté de se noyer?», se demandait-il. Mais pourquoi vouloir user de cette faculté puisque, selon les mots d'un autre écrivain français, Jacques de Lacretelle, la «sérénité familière et encourageante, nulle ville ne la communique mieux que Bruxelles»?

De Kunstberg vormt de scheidingslijn met de rand van de **benedenstad** en grenst nu aan de Albertina of Koninklijke Bibliotheek en het Congrespaleis. Deze lijn loopt tot op het Europakruispunt samen met de Magdalenasteenweg *(voorgrond)*, een straat waarvan de naam teruggaat tot de 17de eeuw, maar waarvan het tracé al dateert uit het prille begin van de Brusselse stadsontwikkeling.

Op de achtergrond, en gebouwd aan de uiterste rand van de bovenstad, domineert het Justitiepaleis *(links)* een groot deel van het panorama. Storend element hierin zijn twee torengebouwen, waarvan er één de klokkentoren van de Kapellekerk, gelegen aan de rand van de Marollen, wel lijkt te willen platdrukken.

Gelukkig bleef de omgeving rond het stadhuis en de Grote Markt *(rechts)* grotendeels bewaard zoals gepland door de Brusselse stadsmagistraat na de bombardementen in 1695.

In de verte liggen de buitenwijken, die het rustieke uitzicht van de vorige eeuw volledig hebben verloren.

Brussel is een stad zonder rivier, wat de Franse schrijver Gérard de Nerval zich verbaasd deed afvragen: "Wat voor hoofdstad is dit, waar men niet eens de mogelijkheid heeft zich te verdrinken?" Volgens een ander Frans schrijver, Jacques de Lacretelle, is die mogelijkheid helemaal niet nodig, aangezien "Brussel een gemoedelijke en aanstekelijke sfeer uitstraalt die in geen andere stad te vinden is."

Now bordered by the Albert I Royal Library and the conference centre, the Mont des Arts touches on the perimeter of the **lower town** which coincides, as far as the Crossroads of Europe, with the Rue de la Madeleine *(foreground)*. The street has borne this name since the 17th century though it dates from the earliest urban development.

In the background, the Law Courts perched on the edge of the upper town *(left)* dominate part of the panorama despite two intrusive towers, one of which seems to want to crush the steeple of the Church de la Chapelle on the edge of the Marolles quarter.

Luckily, the area around the Town Hall and the Grand-Place *(right)* remains much as it was laid out by the Magistrates after the bombardment of 1695.

The suburbs extending into the distance have lost completely the rustic character of the past.

No river crosses the city, which astonished the French author, Gérard de Nerval. "What sort of capital is this, without the possibility to drown oneself?" he asked. But why would one want such a possibility when, according to Jacques de Lacretelle, another French author, "no city exudes better than Brussels a comfortable and cheerful serenity".

Der von der Königlichen Bibliothek Albert I. und dem Kongresspalast begrenzte Mont des Arts markiert die Grenze zwischen Ober- und **Unterstadt**. Bis zum Carrefour de l'Europe verläuft diese Trennungslinie eine Straße entlang, die seit dem 17. Jh. Rue de la Madeleine *(im Vordergrund)* heißt, aber fast so alt ist wie Brüssel selbst.

Der Justizpalast erhebt sich am äußersten Ende der Oberstadt *(links im Hintergrund)*. Er beherrscht noch immer einen Teil des Stadtbilds, obschon zwei ungestalte Hochhäuser, von denen eins den Turm der Kapellenkirche am Rande des Marollenviertels zu erdrücken scheint, ihm seinen Rang neuerdings streitig zu machen versuchen.

Glücklicherweise entspricht der Stadtkern um das Rathaus und den Marktplatz herum *(hier rechts)* noch in großen Zügen dem Plan, den die Stadtväter für den Wiederaufbau nach der Bombardierung von 1695 erstellt hatten.

In der Ferne erstrecken sich die modernen Vorstädte, die im 19. Jh. noch ein völlig ländliches Gepräge trugen.

Es fließt kein Fluss mehr durch die Stadt, was den Dichter Gérard de Nerval zu der Frage veranlasste: "Wie kann es eine Hauptstadt geben, in der man sich nicht einmal ertränken kann?" Einem anderen französischen Schriftsteller, J. de Lacretelle, scheinen derartige Überlegungen ganz fremd zu sein, denn er schreibt: "Keine Stadt strahlt soviel ungezwungene und aufmunternde Heiterkeit aus wie Brüssel."

◁

Œuvre néo-classique de l'architecte Jean-Pierre Cluysenaer, les **galeries Saint-Hubert** furent inaugurées par Léopold Ier en 1847. Leur succès fut immediat; d'emblée elles devinrent le lieu de rendez-vous des gens de bonne société attirés par les théâtres, les magasins et les cafés. Plusieurs architectes étrangers les prirent en modèle, notamment l'Italien Mangoni lorsqu'il dressa les plans de la galerie Victor-Emmanuel à Milan.

De **Sint-Hubertusgalerijen** werden in 1847 door koning Leopold I plechtig geopend. Dit neoklassiek gebouwencomplex, dat door Jean-Pierre Cluysenaer werd ontworpen, had onmiddellijk veel succes. Het werd meteen de ontmoetingsplaats van de welgestelde burgers die weldra voor de charme van de schouwburgen, winkels en cafés bezweken. Ook buitenlandse architecten volgden het Brusselse voorbeeld, o.a. de Italiaan Mangoni, toen hij de plattegrond tekende voor de Vittorio Emmanuele galerij in Milaan.

The neo-classical **covered arcade of St. Hubert**, built by the architect Jean-Pierre Cluysenaer, was opened by Leopold I in 1847. It was an instant success and became the meeting place for both society people, drawn by the theatres, shops and cafés. A number of foreign architects used it as a model, such as Mangoni, an Italian who designed the Victor-Emmanuel arcade in Milan.

Die im neoklassizistischen Stil gebaute **Galerie Saint-Hubert**, ein Werk des Architekten Jean-Pierre Cluysenaer, wurde 1847 von König Leopold I. feierlich eröffnet. Ihr war sofort ein großer Erfolg beschieden, da sie recht schnell zum Treffpunkt der wohlhabenden Bürger wurde, die sich in Schauspielhäusern, Geschäften und Gaststätten trafen. Auch ausländische Architekten fanden Gefallen an dem Konzept, u.a. der Italiener Mangoni, für dessen Galeria Vittor-Emmanuele in Mailand die Brüsseler Galerie Pate stand.

△

La **rue des Bouchers**. Les gastronomes de l'Ancien et du Nouveau monde ne manquent pas d'y déguster, à chaque passage par Bruxelles, les moules blanches comme du lait qui se marient parfaitement avec les frites, la bière ou le vin blanc. Détail curieux, on les sert surtout dans cette rue dédiée aux marchands de viande.

De **Beenhouwersstraat**. Bij elk bezoek aan Brussel denken fijnproevers van de Oude en de Nieuwe wereld er aan om daar de melkwitte mosselen te proeven die zo goed smaken met frieten, bier, of witte wijn. Pittig detail: men serveert de mosselen vooral in deze straat, die aan de vleeshandelaren is opgedragen.

The **Rue des Bouchers** is where the gourmets of the Old and New worlds come when they are in Brussels to savour snowy white mussels complemented with French fries and white wine or beer. Oddly enough they are the speciality of a street named after butchers.

Die **Rue des Bouchers**. Die Feinschmecker des alten und des neuen Kontinents versäumen es nicht, bei jedem Aufenthalt in Brüssel dort die milchweißen Muscheln zu kosten, die perfekt mit den Pommes Frites, dem Bier oder dem Weißwein harmonieren. Kurioserweise werden sie vor allem in dieser Straße serviert, die doch den Fleischern gewidmet ist.

△

Au fond de l'impasse Schuddeveld, qui semble creusée dans la Petite Rue des Bouchers, on decouvre le **Théâtre de Toone**. Ses marionnettes, dont certaines sont devenues pièces de musée, et son répertoire maintiennent vivant le truculent dialecte bruxellois. Les Toone constituent une dynastie où la succession est réglée par la vocation et non pas le sang.

The **Toone Theatre** is situated at the end of Impasse Schuddeveld, a tiny dead-end alley opening off the Petite Rue des Bouchers. Toone's marionettes, some of which are museum pieces, and the repertoire of plays, keep the vigorous Brussels dialect alive. The heir to the Toone dynasty is selected by vocation rather than blood.

De Schuddeveldsteeg, als ingegraven in de Korte Beenhouwersstraat, loopt dood op het **theater van Toone**. Met zijn marionetten, waarvan vele museumstukken geworden zijn, en zijn repertorium houdt dit poppentheater het sappige Brusselse dialect in ere. In de Toone dynastie wordt de opvolging bepaald door roeping en niet door bloedbanden.

Am Ende einer Sackgasse, die den Namen Schuddeveld trägt und die sich in die Petite Rue des Bouchers einzuzwängen scheint, entdeckt der Besucher das **Toone-Theater**. Mit seinen Marionetten, von denen manche Museumwert haben, und seinem Repertoire gewinnt dieses Puppentheater dem urwüchsigen Brüsseler Dialekt immer neue Anhänger. Die Familie Toone ist eine Art Dynastie, in der die Erbfolge nicht durch das Geburtsrecht, sondern durch die künstlerische Berufung bestimmt wird.

Les deux **rues des Bouchers**, la Grande et la Petite, fleurent bon la boustifaille que le poète Eustache Deschamps célébra avec lyrisme au XIVe siècle, en détaillant les sa-veurs des «connins, plouviers et capons, et fesans»...

Le «Savarin» présen-te, rue des Bouchers, une façade baroque en brique et grès de la fin du XVIIe siècle.

In de twee **Been-houwersstraten**, de Grote en de Kleine, geurt het lekker naar vleesgerechten. Reeds in de 14de eeuw bezong de dichter Eustache Deschamps de smeuïge smaak in zijn gedichten, waarin hij het had over "konijnen, plevieren, kapoenen en fazan-ten..."

De "Savarin" in de Beenhouwersstraat heeft een barokke voorgevel in bak- en zandsteen van het eind van de 17de eeuw.

The two **Rues des Bouchers**, both big and little, are great for the sort of nosh that the poet Eustache De-schamps rhapsodized about in the 14th cen-tury, detailing mouth-watering, "rabbits, plovers, capons and pheasants".

The "Savarin" on the Rue des Bouchers has a late 17th century brick and sandstone façade.

Sowohl in der gro-ßen als auch in der kleinen **Rue des Bouchers** (Metzger-straße) riecht es ange-nehm nach den Fleischgerichten, deren Geschmack der Dich-ter Eustache schon im 14. Jh. in seinen Gedichten über "Ka-ninchen, Regenpfeifer, Kapaune und Fasane" rühmte.

Das "Savarin"-Haus in der Rue des Bou-chers weist eine vom Ende des 17. Jahr-hunderts stammende Barockfassade aus Back- und Sandstein auf.

Tracée dès le XIᵉ siècle, la rue au Beurre relie la Grand-Place à l'église Saint-Nicolas. Elle doit son appellation au marché qui s'y tint jusqu'en 1798. La maison qui y porte le numéro 31 s'appelle joliment «**De Peerle**». Elle est comme nimbée d'un parfum de pâtisserie. En effet, depuis 1829, l'une des plus anciennes familles de Bruxelles y offre aux gourmets les plus délicieux biscuits bruxellois. En particulier les speculoos, d'une «pâte faite de farine, beurre, cassonade, canelle en poudre, œufs, clous de girofle» et dont on «fait de petits gâteaux sur des formes les plus diverses».

(À droite)
Une série de maisons sont accolées à l'**église Saint-Nicolas**. Celle qui est implantée de biais fut reconstruite à partir des éléments d'une jolie demeure de la rue de l'Étuve. L'église gothique dédiée au patron des bateliers – l'ancien port sur la Senne n'était pas loin – a perdu sa tour, qui s'est écroulée en 1714.

De Boterstraat bestond reeds in de 11de eeuw en verbindt de Grote Markt met de Sint-Nikolaaskerk. Ze heeft haar naam te danken aan de markt die er tot 1798 werd gehouden. Het huis met nummer 31 draagt de mooie naam "**De Peerle**". Het lijkt wel gehuld in een wolk van patisserie. Sinds 1829 maakt één van de oudste families van Brussel daar inderdaad de lekkerste Brusselse koekjes. Vooral de speculoos, een "deeg van bloem, boter, bruine suiker, kaneelpoeder, eieren en kruidnagel waaruit men kleine koekjes in de meest diverse vormen maakt", is in trek.

(Rechts)
Een rij huizen leunt tegen de **Sint-Nikolaaskerk**. Het dwarsstaande huis werd gereconstrueerd met elementen van een mooie woning in de Stoofstraat. De gotische kerk is opgedragen aan de patroonheilige van de binnenschippers – de oude haven aan de Zenne was niet veraf. De kerk verloor haar toren toen die in 1714 instortte.

The Rue au Beurre, dating from the 11th century, links the Grand-Place to Saint Nicholas' church. It takes its name from the butter market held there until 1798. From the house numbered 31, called "**The Pearl**", floats a heavenly aroma of baking. Since 1829 one of the oldest Brussels families has offered gourmets the most delicious Brussels cookies, especially the speculoos of a "dough made of flour, butter, brown sugar, cinnamon, eggs and cloves" made into "little cakes in many shapes".

(Above)
A series of houses abut the church of **Saint Nicholas**. The one at an angle was rebuilt with pieces from a pretty house on the Rue de l'Étuve. The Gothic church dedicated to the patron saint of the boatmen – the former port on the Senne was nearby – has lost its tower that collapsed in 1714.

Die bereits im 11. Jahrhundert gezogene Rue au Beurre (Butterstraße) verbindet die Grand-Place mit der St.-Nikolaus Kirche. Sie verdankt ihre Bezeichnung dem Markt, der dort bis 1798 abgehalten wurde. Das Haus mit der Nummer 31 trägt den hübschen Namen **"De Peerle"**. Es scheint in Konditoreiduft eingehüllt zu sein. In der Tat bietet hier seit 1829 eine der ältesten Familien Brüssels den Feinschmeckern die köstlichsten Brüsseler Kekse an, insbesondere die Speculoos, hergestellt aus einem "Teig aus Mehl, Butter, Rohzucker, Zimtpulver, Eiern, Gewürznelke", woraus man dann "kleine Kuchen in den verschiedensten Formen backt".

(Oben)
Eine Reihe von Häusern lehnen sich an die **St.-Nikolaus Kirche** an. Das schräg errichtete Gebäude wurde unter Verwendung von Bauteilen einer schönen Wohnstätte in der Rue de l'Étuve rekonstruiert. Die dem Schutzpatron der Schiffer gewidmete gotische Kirche – der alte Hafen an der Senne war nicht weit – hat ihren Turm verloren, der im Jahre 1714 zusammenstürzte.

Comparée à un riche théâtre par Jean Cocteau, la **Grand-Place** séduit par son exceptionnelle unité architecturale. Celle-ci n'est pas fortuite. Deux ans après le bombardement de 1695, le Magistrat prit une ordonnance imposant l'approbation préalable des plans de toute reconstruction. La juxtaposition des édifices se fit, dès lors, sous le signe de l'harmonie parfaite entre les projets individuels.

Door haar uitzonderlijke architecturale eenheid heeft de **Grote Markt** reeds velen bekoord. Zo ook Jean Cocteau, die haar vergeleek met een groots schouwtoneel. Die eenheid kwam echter niet toevallig tot stand. Twee jaar na het bombardement van 1695 vaardigde de stadsmagistraat een verordening uit waardoor elk reconstructieplan vooraf moest worden goedgekeurd. Op die manier kwam een perfecte harmonie tot stand tussen de naast elkaar geplaatste individuele bouwwerken.

The **Grand-Place** with its exceptional architectural unity was described by Jean Cocteau as "an opulent theatre". Two years after the bombardment of 1695 the Magistrate ordained that prior approval of plans had to be obtained before any reconstruction. Perfect harmony in the placement of the buildings was thus achieved.

Die einzigartige architektonische Einheitlichkeit der **Grand-Place**, die Jean Cocteau mit einer prächtig ausgestatteten Bühne verglich, hat sich keineswegs zufällig ergeben. Zwei Jahre nach der Bombardierung von 1695 erließ der Stadtrat einen Beschluss, der alle Rekonstruktionsvorhaben genehmigungspflichtig machte. Dies hatte die Abstimmung der individuellen Baupläne auf ein ausgewogenes Gesamtkonzept zur Folge.

△▷
Les corporations bruxelloises jouèrent un rôle essentiel, non seulement dans la vie économique de la ville mais aussi dans sa vie politique. Leurs interventions, parfois les armes à la main, furent souvent décisives. Rien ne pourrait mieux l'évoquer que leurs drapeaux qui ajoutent aux dorures des façades de la Grand-Place l'éclat de leurs couleurs vives.

La bannière des merciers flotte sur **Le Renard**, la maison de cette corporation; elle est l'œuvre de l'architecte Corneille Van Neven et dresse cinq statues de J. Dillens devant le trumeau du premier étage. Celle du milieu symbolise la Justice, sans doute par allusion au respect des lois qui s'impose à tous les marchands. Les quatre autres évoquent l'Afrique, l'Europe, l'Asie et l'Amérique.

Les angelots grassouillets qui s'agitent sur la frise témoignent, avec leur charme naturel, de l'apport italien dans la décoration des maisons de la Grand-Place.

The guilds of Brussels played an important role in both the economic and political life of the City, and their actions – sometimes armed – were often decisive. Nothing evokes their days of glory better than their gaily coloured flags which float before the gilded facades of the Grand-Place.

The Haberdashers banner waves in front of their guild house, **The Fox**, built by Corneille van Neven. Five statues by J. Dillens ornament the piers of the first storey with Justice in the middle, doubtless alluding to the Law which all merchants must respect. The four others represent Africa, Europe, Asia and America.

The chubby cherubs frolicking on the frieze demonstrate Italian influence on the decoration of the houses of the Grand-Place.

De Brusselse gilden speelden een essentiële rol, niet enkel op economisch maar ook op politiek vlak. Hun tussenkomst, soms zelfs gewapenderhand, was vaak doorslaggevend. Niets geeft een duidelijker idee van hun macht dan de felle kleuren van hun vlaggen, die het verguldsel op de gevels van de Grote Markt nog beter doen uitkomen.

De vlag van de garen- en bandwerkverkopers wappert voor de gevels van **Den Vos**, het huis van deze gilde. Het gebouw werd door bouwmeester Cornelius van Neven ontworpen en op de steunpilaren van de eerste verdieping staan vijf gebeeldhouwde figuren van J. Dillens. De gestalte in het midden stelt de gerechtigheid voor, waarschijnlijk een verwijzing naar de eerbied die alle kooplui de wet verschuldigd zijn; de vier andere zijn allegorieën van Afrika, Europa, Azië en Amerika.

De bekoorlijkheid en de gracieuze natuurlijkheid van de mollige engeltjes op de fries getuigen van de Italiaanse invloed op de siermotieven die de huizen rond de Grote Markt verfraaien.

Nicht nur im wirtschaftlichen, auch im politischen Leben spielten die Zünfte der Stadt eine kaum zu überschätzende Rolle. Wenn sie, ob bewaffnet oder nicht, einschritten, war dies oft ausschlaggebend. Nichts vermag ihre Macht deutlicher vor Augen zu führen als die grellen Farben ihrer Fahnen, die den vergoldeten Häuserfassaden am Marktplatz noch mehr Glanz verleihen.

Die Fahne der Kurzwarenhändler flattert vor **dem Fuchs**, dem Haus dieser Zunft. Der Baumeister Cornelius Van Neven errichtete es. Auf den Fensterpfeilern des ersten Stockwerks stehen fünf Statuen von J. Dillens. In der Mitte steht die Gerechtigkeit (wohl ein Hinweis auf die von den Kaufleuten geforderte Achtung vor dem Gesetz) und, ihr zur Rechten und zur Linken, stehen die Allegorien Afrikas, Europas, Asiens und Amerikas.

Die rundlichen Engelchen auf dem Fries weisen mit ihrer ungekünstelten Grazie auf die aus Italien stammenden Einflüsse hin, die das äußere Erscheinungsbild der Häuser des Marktplatzes mitbestimmt haben.

Les boulangers n'utilisèrent que pendant peu de temps la Halle au Pain qui, dès le XVe siècle, abrita des services administratifs du duc de Brabant. Celui-ci deviendra roi d'Espagne à partir du XVIe siècle. D'où le nom de **Maison du Roi** *(à gauche)*, qu'aucun souverain n'habita jamais. Fortement inspiré de l'hôtel de ville d'Audenarde, le bâtiment actuel date de la fin du XIXe siècle.

La **Maison des Ducs de Brabant** *(à l'arrière-plan)* se compose en réalité de six maisons parfaitement semblables, sommées depuis 1770 d'un fronton arrondi. Les bustes en pierre au premier étage représentent les ducs de Brabant.

Tous les deux ans, vers la mi-août, la Grand-Place se pare d'un somptueux et éphémère tapis de bégonias.

De bakkers maakten slechts kortstondig gebruik van de Broodhalle die in de 15de eeuw onderdak bood aan de administratieve diensten van de hertog van Brabant, die vanaf de 16de eeuw koning van Spanje werd. Toch wordt dit gebouw nog steeds het **Broodhuis** *(links)* genoemd. Het huidige gebouw dateert van het einde van de 19de eeuw en is sterk geïnspireerd op het stadhuis van Oudenaarde.

Het **Huis van de Hertogen van Brabant** *(op de achtergrond)* is in werkelijkheid een geheel van zes identieke huizen, die sinds 1770 een afgerond fronton dragen. De stenen borstbeelden op de eerste verdieping stellen de hertogen van Brabant voor.

Om de twee jaar tooit de Grote Markt zich rond half augustus met een prachtig, maar vergankelijk begoniatapijt.

The bakers used their bread market but for a short while and from the 15th century on the building served as the administrative offices of the Duke of Brabant, who became the King of Spain in the 16th century. Hence the name the **King's House** *(left)*. Though the architecture is strongly influenced by that of the town hall of Oudenaarde the present building dates from the end of the 19th century.

The **House of the Dukes of Brabant** *(background)* is actually made up of six identical houses crowned in 1770 by a curved pediment. The stone busts on the first storey represent Dukes of Brabant.

Every two years around mid-August the Grand-Place is decorated with a sumptuous and ephemeral carpet of begonias.

Die Bäcker nutzten die Brothalle nur kurze Zeit, in der sich ab dem 15. Jahrhundert dann die Verwaltungsräume des Herzogs von Brabant befanden, der im 16. Jahrhundert König von Spanien wurde. Daher der Name **Haus des Königs** *(links)*, das doch niemals von einem Herrscher bewohnt wurde. Das heutige Gebäude stammt vom Ende des 19. Jahrhunderts; es ist architektonisch stark vom Rathaus von Audenarde geprägt.

Das **Haus der Herzöge von Brabant** *(im Hintergrund)* setzt sich in Wirklichkeit aus sechs völlig gleichen Häusern zusammen, die seit 1770 von einem abgerundeten Frontgiebel bedeckt sind. Die Steinbüsten im ersten Stockwerk stellen die Herzöge von Brabant dar.

Alle zwei Jahre wird Mitte August die Grand-Place mit einem prachtvollen und vergänglichen Teppich aus Begonien geschmückt.

CRESCIT EUNDO

Une Renommée surmonte la septième porte de la **Maison des Ducs de Brabant**, au coin de la rue des Chapeliers.
Les disciples les plus fervents de Gambrinus se sont toujours rencontrés à Bruxelles, où sont brassées plusieurs bières locales. Seule la corporation des Brasseurs possède toujours sa maison à la Grand-Place, **l'Arbre d'Or,** que couronne la statue équestre de Charles de Lorraine, le bien-aimé et le bon vivant. Les bas-reliefs chantent les vendanges et la cueillette du houblon.

Op de hoek van de Hoedenmakersstraat prijkt boven de zevende deur van het **Huis van de Hertogen van Brabant** een standbeeldje van de godin Fama.
Brussel, waar talrijke lokale biersoorten worden gebrouwen, is sinds mensenheugnis de ontmoetingsplaats geweest voor de meest fervente aanhangers van Gambrinus. Enkel de brouwersgilde bezit nog steeds een eigen huis op de Grote Markt: **de Gouden Boom.** Het wordt bekroond door het ruiterstandbeeld van Karel van Lorreinen, de populaire levensgenieter. De basreliëfs bezingen de wijnoogst en het plukken van de hop.

The goddess Fame can be seen over the seventh door of the **House of the Dukes of Brabant,** at the corner of the Rue des Chapeliers.
Fervent followers of Gambrinus, the mythical Flemish king who is supposed to have invented beer, have always met in Brussels where a number of local beers are brewed. The Brewers' guild is the only one still in occupation of its house in the Grand-Place, **the Golden Tree,** which is topped with an equestrian statue of Charles of Lorraine, a easy-going sovereign.

An der Ecke der Rue des Chapeliers thront eine Statue der Fama über dem **Hof der Herzöge von Brabant**.
In Brüssel, wo mehrere nur örtlich bekannte Biersorten gebraut werden, hat es Gambrinus nie an treuen Anhängern gefehlt. Allein die Gilde der Brauer besitzt noch immer ihr Haus auf dem Großen Markt, **den Goldenen Baum,** den das Reiterstandbild Karls von Lothringen, des volkstümlichen Fürsten, krönt.

C'est au printemps de 1412 que fut posée la première pierre de l'aile gauche de l'**hôtel de ville**. Quarante ans plus tard, le futur Charles le Téméraire posait la première pierre de l'aile droite et il parut alors que l'ancienne tour était minable et manquait de verticalité. En 1449, la ville chargea l'architecte Jean van Ruysbroeck d'ériger une tour monumentale, véritable dentelle de pierre qui surgit du sol d'un seul jet de nonante mètres de hauteur.
(Ci-dessus)
De la décoration originale du **Cabinet du Bourgmestre** (1718) dans l'hôtel de ville, seul subsiste le plafond. La restauration de 1890 s'est faite dans le style Louis XIV. Sur les murs, une double rangée de tableaux de François Stroobant représente des monuments anciens de la ville.

The foundation stone of the left wing of the **Town Hall** was laid in 1412. Forty years later when the future Charles the Bold laid the foundation stone of the right wing it was felt that the old tower was not imposing enough and in 1449 Jean van Ruysbroeck was commissioned by the city to build a more magnificent one. The tower, rising nearly 90 meters from ground level appears to be made of stone lace.
(Above)
Only the ceiling of 1718 remains of the original decor of the **Mayor's office** in the Town Hall; the 1890 restoration is in the style of Louis XIV. On the walls hang a double row of pictures by François Stroobant depicting old city monuments.

In de lente van 1412 had de eerstesteenlegging plaats van de linkervleugel van het **stadhuis**. Veertig jaar later legde de latere Karel de Stoute de grondsteen voor de rechtervleugel. Toen bleek de oude toren er te armzalig uit te zien en op de koop toe ook nog scheefgegroeid te zijn. In 1449 belastte het stadsbestuur bouwmeester Jan van Ruysbroeck met de bouw van een grootse toren. Het werd een echt kantwerk van steen dat tot een hoogte van 90 meter omhoogrijst.
(Hierboven)
Van de oorspronkelijke interieurversiering van het **kabinet van de burgemeester** (1718) in het stadhuis is alleen de zolderschildering bewaard gebleven. In 1890 werd het kabinet in Lodewijk XIV-stijl gerestaureerd. De muren zijn door Frans Stroobant met een dubbele rij oude stadsgebouwen en -gezichten beschilderd.

Im Frühling 1412 wurde der Grundstein zum linken Flügel des **Rathauses** gelegt. Vierzig Jahre danach nahm der spätere Karl der Kühne die Grundsteinlegung zum rechten Flügel vor. Da wurde die Unangepasstheit und die Schiefheit des alten Turms vollends augenfällig. Deshalb beauftragte die Stadtverwaltung Jean van Ruysbroeck 1449 mit dem Bau eines monumentalen Turmes, dessen Grundpfeiler in kühnem Schwung bis zu einer Höhe von 90 m emporschießen und in eine kunstvoll aus Stein gewirkte Spitzendraperie gehüllt sind.
(Oben)
Von der ursprünglichen Ausstattung der **Amtsstube des Bürgermeisters** (1718) im Rathaus ist bei der Restaurierung von 1890 im Louis XIV-Stil nur das Deckengemälde verschont geblieben. Auf die Wände malte F. Stroobant in doppelreihiger Anordnung Skizzen der ältesten Gebäude der Stadt.

Au XIVe siècle, un petit garçon prénommé Juliaanske aurait éteint en urinant la mèche allumée d'une bombe destinée à mettre le feu à Bruxelles. Ce serait, selon certains, l'origine de la statuette de **Manneken-Pis** que Jérôme Duquesnoy sculpta en 1619 pour orner l'angle des rues du Chêne et de l'Étuve.

(À droite)

Les moines qui s'y étaient fixés en 1249 ont donné leur nom à la **rue des Grands Carmes**; leur couvent fut rasé par les révolutionnaires français en 1795. À l'ombre de l'église Notre-Dame de Bon Secours, plusieurs façades – l'une d'elles, baroque, date de 1696 – ont été débarrassées du crépis qui les dissimulait. C'est symbolique d'une revitalisation de tout le quartier où jeunes et moins jeunes branchés se réunissent volontiers dans les «cafés-restos» qui s'y sont multipliés.

In de 14de eeuw zou een klein jongentje, Juliaanske, al waterend de brandende lont hebben gedoofd van een bom die heel Brussel in brand had moeten steken. Volgens sommigen ligt hierin de oorsprong van het standbeeldje van **Manneken-Pis** dat Jérôme Duquesnoy in 1619 maakte en dat nu prijkt op de hoek van de Eikstraat en de Stoofstraat.

(Links)

De **Lievevrouwbroersstraat** dankt haar naam aan de monniken die er zich in 1249 vestigden; hun klooster werd met de grond gelijk gemaakt door de Franse revolutionairen in 1795. In de schaduw van de Onze-Lieve-Vrouw van Bijstandkerk vindt men verschillende voorgevels – één ervan, in barokstijl, dateert van 1696 – waarvan de pleisterlaag werd afgehaald om ze in hun oorspronkelijke staat te herstellen. Dit is symbolisch voor de herleving van de hele wijk, waar een jong en minder jong hip volkje zich graag laat zien in de talrijke "café-restos".

In the 14th century a little boy named Juliaanske is said to have extinguished the burning fuse of a bomb meant to blow up Brussels by urinating on it. The little statue of **Manneken-Pis**, sculpted by Jerome Duquesnoy in 1619 to decorate the corner of the angle of the Rue du Chêne and Rue de l'Étuve, is supposed to commemorate this deed.

(Right)

The **Rue des Grands Carmes** is named after the monks who settled there in 1249. Their monastery was razed by French revolutionaries in 1795. In the shadow of the church of Our Lady of Good Help several façades – the baroque one dates from 1696 – have been cleaned of the roughcast which covered them. This is symbolic of the whole district where the young – and not-so-young – swingers gladly meet in the bistros that have sprung up.

Im 14. Jh. soll ein kleiner, Juliaanske heißender Junge die schon brennende Zündschnur einer Bombe, die Brüssel in Brand stecken sollte, gelöscht haben, indem er ausgiebig darauf pinkelte. Dies soll Jérôme Duquesnoy 1619 zu der kleinen Bronzestatue von **Manneken-Pis** inspiriert haben, die nun an der Ecke der Rue du Chêne und der Rue de l'Étuve steht.

(Rechts)

Die Mönche, die sich im Jahre 1249 dort niedergelassen hatten, gaben der **Rue des Grands Carmes** (Straße der Karmeliter) ihren Namen; ihr Kloster wurde von den französischen Revolutionären 1795 zerstört. Im Schatten der Kirche Notre-Dame de Bon Secours wurden mehrere Fassaden – darunter eine Barockfassade aus dem Jahre 1696 – vom Putz befreit, unter dem sie versteckt lagen. Dies ist symbolisch für die Wiederbelebung eines ganzen Viertels, in dem junge und weniger junge Leute im Trend ihrer Zeit sich gerne in den "Café-Restaurants" treffen, die dort in großer Zahl eröffnet worden sind.

△

Commencée en 1666, l'**église Notre-Dame de Bon Secours** remplaçait une modeste chapelle sur la route du pèlerinage de Saint-Jacques de Compostelle. On y vénérait une statuette de la Vierge découverte en 1625, à laquelle le petit peuple, soutenu par l'archiduchesse Isabelle, avait promptement attribué des vertus miraculeuses. La façade Renaissance est l'œuvre de l'architecte Pierre-Paul Merckx; elle fut terminée en 1694, un an avant le bombardement de Bruxelles qui endommagea gravement l'église.

Begun in 1666 the **church of Our Lady of Good Help** replaced a modest chapel on the pilgrimage route to Santiago de Compostela. A statuette of the virgin discovered in 1625 was venerated there. The common people, seconded by Archduchess Isabella had immediately attributed miraculous powers to it. The Renaissance façade was the work of the architect Peter-Paul Merckx and was finished in 1694, one year before the bombardment of Brussels when the church was badly damaged.

Met de bouw van de **Onze-Lieve-Vrouw van Bijstandkerk** werd gestart in 1666. Ze verving een bescheiden kapel op de pelgrims-route naar Sint-Jacobus van Compostela. Men aanbad er een beeldje van de Heilige Maagd, ontdekt in 1625, waaraan het gewone volk, gesteund door de aartshertogin Isabella, al snel miraculeuze krachten toeschreef. De Renaissance-voorgevel is het werk van architect Pieter-Paulus Merckx; ze werd afgewerkt in 1694, één jaar voor het bombardement op Brussel dat de kerk zwaar beschadigde.

Der 1666 begonnene **Kirchenbau Notre-Dame de Bon Secours** wurde an der Stelle einer einfachen Kapelle auf dem Pilgerweg nach Santiago de Compostela errichtet. Man verehrte dort eine kleine, im Jahre 1625 gefundene Statue der Jungfrau Maria, der das einfache Volk unterstützt durch die Erzherzogin Isabella sofort wundertätige Eigenschaften zuschrieb. Die Renaissancefassade ist das Werk des Architekten Pieter-Paulus Merckx; sie wurde im Jahre 1694 beendet, ein Jahr vor der Bombardierung Brüssels, bei der die Kirche schwer beschädigt wurde.

Religieuses cloîtrées, les Riches Claires étaient dotées d'un revenu annuel, d'où leur nom. Il leur était interdit de mendier. Ce qui n'a jamais empêché les fidèles de leur offrir des œufs dans l'espoir que leurs fêtes de mariage ou de communion ne soient pas gâchées par la pluie... Entre 1665 et 1680, elles firent édifier une église baroque par le sculpteur et architecte malinois Luc Fayd'Herbe. Incendiée en 1989, l'**église Notre-Dame aux Riches Claires** a retrouvé presque toute sa décoration originelle. Les arcs doubleaux des voûtes présentent des bossages très marqués, tout comme les arcs qui soutiennent la coupole; des anges en stucs ornent les pendentifs de celle-ci.

De Rijke Klaren waren kloosterreligieuzen die een jaarlijks inkomen kregen, vandaar hun naam. Het was hen niet toegestaan te bedelen, maar dat heeft hun aanhangers er nooit van weerhouden hen eieren te schenken in de hoop dat hun huwelijks- of communiefeesten niet door regen werden verstoord... Tussen 1665 en 1680 lieten zij een barokke kerk optrekken door de Mechelse beeldhouwer en architect Lucas Fayd'Herbe. Hoewel in de **kerk van Onze-Lieve-Vrouw van de Rijke Klaren** in 1989 brand werd gesticht, is haar oorspronkelijke decoratie bijna volledig hersteld. De gewelfribben zijn rijkelijk versierd, evenals de gewelfbogen die de koepel ondersteunen; engelen in stucwerk decoreren het gewelfzwik.

The Riches Claires, cloistered nuns of the order of Saint Clare, were given an annual income as they were forbidden to beg, whence their name. This did not stop the faithful from giving them eggs in the hope that their marriage or communion festivities would not be spoiled by rain. Between 1665 and 1680 they had a baroque church built by the Mechelen sculptor and architect Lucas Fayd'Herbe. The **church of Our Lady of the Riches Claires** was badly damaged by fire in 1989 but most of its original décor has now been restored. The transverse ribs of the vault present very prominent bosses, like the arches supporting the cupola. The pendentives are decorated with stucco angels.

Die in einem Kloster lebenden Nonnen des Ordens Riches Claires besaßen ein Jahreseinkommen, daher ihr Name "reiche Claires". Das Betteln war ihnen verboten. Dies hatte jedoch niemals die Gläubigen daran gehindert, ihnen Eier zu schenken, damit ihre Hochzeit oder Kommunion nicht durch Regenwetter vermiest würde... Zwischen 1665 und 1680 ließen sie vom Bildhauer und Architekten Lucas Fayd'Herbe aus Mecheln eine barocke Kirche erbauen. Nach einem Brand im Jahre 1989 wurde in der **Kirche Notre-Dame aux Riches Claires** beinahe das gesamte ursprüngliche Dekor wieder hergestellt. Die Gurtbögen der Gewölbe weisen sehr ausgeprägte Bossen auf, ebenso wie die Bögen, die die Kuppel stützen; Engel aus Stuck zieren deren Pendentife.

(Ci-dessus et page 100)
De l'**ancien port de Bruxelles** sur Senne, cœur économique de la cité, il ne subsiste que quelques bassins aménagés entre le Quai aux Briques et le Quai au Bois à Brûler. À leur extrémité, un monument assez hétéroclite, en forme de fontaine-obélisque surmontée d'un saint Michel en bronze doré, a été dressé en l'honneur de Jules Anspach, bourgmestre de Bruxelles de 1864 à 1879.

(Hierboven en blz. 100)
Van de **oude haven van Brussel** aan de Zenne, eertijds het economisch hart van de stad, blijven nog slechts een paar dokken over tussen de Baksteenkaai en de Brandhoutkaai. Aan het uiteinde hiervan staat een nogal heterocliet monument – half fontein, half obelisk – bekroond met een vergulde bronzen Sint-Michiel. Het werd opgericht ter ere van Jules Anspach, die van 1864 tot 1879 burgemeester van Brussel was.

(Above and page 100)
Only a few docks remain, between the Quai aux Briques and the Quai au Bois à Brûler, of the **old port of Brussels** on the Senne, once the economic heart of the city. A rather incongruous monument, a sort of fountain-obelisk crowned by a gilded bronze statue of St. Michael, has been erected in honour of Jules Anspach, mayor of Brussels from 1864 to 1879, at the far end.

(Oben und S. 100)
Vom **alten Hafen Brüssels** an der Senne, früher einmal Mittelpunkt des wirtschaftlichen Lebens der Stadt, bleiben nur noch ein paar Docks zwischen dem Quai aux Briques und dem Quai au Bois à Brûler übrig. Am äußersten Ende der Anlage erhebt sich ein seltsames Monument – zugleich Fontäne und Obelisk –, auf dem eine vergoldete Bronzestatue des Erzengels Michael thront. Es wurde zu Ehren Jules Anspachs errichtet, der von 1864 bis 1879 Bürgermeister Brüssels war.

△

L'imposante **Maison de la Bellone** fut édifiée en 1697 en souvenir de la bataille de Zanta remportée deux ans plus tôt par les Autrichiens sur les Turcs. Ce remarquable immeuble patricien, dont le style classique n'est pas sans analogie avec celui du *Roi d'Espagne* de la Grand-Place, était à l'abandon dans la populeuse rue de Flandre lorsque sa restauration fut entreprise. Recouvert d'une verrière protectrice depuis 1995, il est désormais une très vivante Maison du spectacle.

The imposing **House of Bellona**, named after the Roman goddess of war, was built in 1697 to commemorate the defeat, two years earlier, of the Turks by the Austrians at the Battle of Zanta. This remarkable patrician building, similar in style to *The King of Spain* on the Grand-Place, long stood deserted in the busy Rue de Flandre until its restoration was undertaken. Enveloped in a protective glass covering in 1995, it is now a lively and interesting theater arts centre.

Het indrukwekkende **Bellonahuis** werd in 1697 gebouwd ter herinnering aan de slag van Zanta, waar de Oostenrijkers twee jaar voordien de Turken hadden verslagen. Deze opvallende patriciërswoonst in classicistische stijl toont nogal wat overeenkomsten met *Den Coninck van Spagniën* op de Grote Markt. Het gebouw stond lange tijd verwaarloosd in de drukke Vlaanderenstraat, tot tussen 1965 en 1975 de restauratie werd aangevat. Sinds 1995 wordt het overkoepeld door een glazen beschermkap en is het een springlevend Huis der Toneelkunst.

Das eindrucksvolle **Bellona-Haus** wurde 1697 errichtet. Es soll, wie die darauf Bezug nehmenden Trophäen über der Eingangspforte zeigen, an die Schlacht von Zanta erinnern, in der die Österreicher zwei Jahre zuvor die Türken besiegt hatten. Dieses in klassischem Stil gebaute Patrizierhaus in der belebten Rue de Flandre ist u.a. auch wegen der Ähnlichkeiten bemerkenswert, die es mit *zum König von Spanien* am Marktplatz aufweist. Es war dem völligen Verfall nahe, als es restauriert wurde. Das seit 1995 mit Glas überdachte Gebäude ist inzwischen das sehr rege Haus der Schauspielkunst geworden.

Le **quai aux Briques** a maintenu intacte sa vocation de marché aux poissons. Les restaurants renommés, spécialement en fruits de mer, y déploient leurs tentation multiples.

The **Quai aux Briques** has retained its vocation as a fish market with renowned restaurants specializing in tempting seafood.

De **Baksteenkaai** is trouw gebleven aan haar oorspronkelijke functie van vismarkt. Gerenommeerde restaurants, vooral in zeevruchten, tonen er hun talrijke verleidingen.

Der **Quai aux Briques** hat seine Bestimmung als Fischmarkt beibehalten. Die besonders für ihre Meeresfrüchte berühmten Restaurants präsentieren dort ihre zahlreichen kulinarischen Versuchungen.

△△ Construite selon les plans de Léon Suys qui s'inspira de l'architecture palladienne, la monumentale **Bourse** de Bruxelles fut inaugurée en 1873. Ses façades sont surchargées d'ornements symbolisant le travail, l'industrie et le commerce; Auguste Rodin et Julien Dillens collaborèrent à la charmante frise des amours artisans, sur le côté sud. Le vaisseau intérieur comporte une décoration surabondante.

Built to Palladian-inspired plans by Léon Suys the monumental Brussels **Stock Exchange** was opened in 1873. The façades are heavily ornamented with sculptures symbolizing work, industry and commerce. Auguste Rodin and Julien Dillens worked together on a charming frieze of artisan cupids on the south side. The interior is lavishly decorated.

De monumentale **Beurs** van Brussel werd gebouwd volgens de plannen van Léon Suys, die zich liet inspireren door de palladium-architectuur, en werd in 1873 ingehuldigd. De voorgevels zijn overladen met ornamenten die het werk, de industrie en de handel symboliseren; Auguste Rodin en Julien Dillens werkten samen aan de charmante fries van de artistieke liefde, op de zuidkant. Het binnenschip is zeer overvloedig gedecoreerd.

Die monumentale **Börse** von Brüssel wurde nach den Plänen von Léon Suys erbaut, der sich von der Palladium-Architektur inspirieren ließ, und im Jahre 1873 eingeweiht. Ihre Fassaden sind mit Ornamenten überladen, die Arbeit, die Industrie und den Handel symbolisieren; Auguste Rodin und Julien Dillens arbeiteten an dem bezaubernden Fries der Handwerkerlieben auf der Südseite mit. Das Innenschiff ist überreichlich geschmückt.

△▷▷

Le caractère pittoresque de la Senne d'antan ne compensait pas son insalubrité. À chaque période de crue, elle inondait son environnement, forçant les habitants à évacuer leurs maisons ou à vivre dans la boue. Un an avant l'épidémie de choléra de 1866, le conseil communal décida le voûtement des différents bras de la rivière sur environ deux kilomètres de longueur. Les travaux furent terminés en automne 1871. Au-dessus du voûtement, un large boulevard s'étend depuis le boulevard du Midi jusqu'à l'actuelle **place de Brouckère** où il se divise en deux branches. L'une, établie sur la rivière voûtée, se termine à la hauteur du boulevard d'Anvers, l'autre s'achève devant la place Rogier. Plus de mille maisons avaient disparu mais un nouveau Bruxelles était né.

The picturesque character of the Senne of yesteryear did not compensate for its insalubrity. When it was in spate and overflowed its banks the inhabitants were forced to flee their homes or dwell in the mud. A year before the cholera epidemic of 1866 the municipal council decided to vault over the various arms of the river on a distance of some two kilometers. The works were finished in the autumn of 1871. A wide boulevard extending from the Boulevard du Midi to the present **Place de Brouckère** where it branches in two, runs above this vaulting. One branch continues on to the Boulevard d'Anvers while the other terminates at Place Rogier. More than a thousand houses were razed to build this new Brussels.

Het schilderachtige karakter van de Zenne woog ook vroeger niet op tegen de vervuiling. Bij hoogwater werd de omgeving overstroomd, en de inwoners werden uit hun huizen gedreven of gedwongen in de modder te leven. Een jaar voor de cholera epidemie van 1866, besloot de gemeenteraad tot de overwelving van de verschillende rivierarmen over een afstand van ongeveer 2 km. De werkzaamheden duurden tot in de herfst van 1871. Daarna werd de noord-zuidverkeersader aangelegd : de Zuidlaan, die zich op het huidige **de Brouckèreplein** in tweeën splitst. Een van die aftakkingen volgt de overwelfde rivier tot op de Antwerpselaan, terwijl de tweede op het Rogierplein uitloopt. Meer dan duizend huizen waren ondertussen gesloopt en het stadsbeeld was ingrijpend veranderd.

Die wohl recht malerischen Mäander der Senne verwandelten sich in früheren Zeiten oft in gefährliche Infektionsherde. Kam es zu Überschwemmungen, dann mussten die Leute ausziehen oder mit dem Schlamm vorlieb nehmen. Ein Jahr vor der Choleraepidemie von 1866 beschloss der Stadtrat die Überwölbung des Flusses auf einer Strecke von etwa 2 km. Die Arbeiten dauerten bis 1871. Über dem Fluss erstreckt sich nun der Boulevard du Midi, der sich **Place de Brouckère** gabelt, wobei eine Verzweigung dem Bett der Senne bis zum Boulevard nach Antwerpen folgt, während die zweite Richtung Rogierplatz verläuft. Inzwischen waren mehr als tausend Häuser von der Bildfläche verschwunden, und Brüssel hatte sich stark verändert.

Peu d'opéras européens peuvent se vanter d'un passé et d'un présent aussi rayonnants que ceux du **Théâtre Royal de la Monnaie**. Le bâtiment actuel de style néo-classique – sauf ses récentes adjonctions – date de 1819. Après l'incendie qui ravagea le théâtre le 21 janvier 1855, une toute nouvelle salle fut réalisée par l'architecte Poelaert, dans le style le plus riche du XVIIe siècle. Elle est de forme elliptique et se trouve, en quelque sorte, prolongée par le plafond.

Slechts weinig Europese operagebouwen kunnen bogen op zo'n schitterend verleden en heden als de **Koninklijke Muntschouwburg**. Het huidige theater dateert van 1819 en heeft een neoklassieke stijl, afgezien van de recente toevoegingen. Nadat een brand op 21 januari 1855 de Muntschouwburg had verwoest, werd Poelaert met de bouw en de architectonische versiering van een geheel nieuwe zaal belast. Dit prachtwerk in 17de-eeuwse stijl heeft de vorm van een ellips die tot in de hanenbalken omhoogrijst.

Few opera-houses in Europe can pride themselves on such a prestigious past and present as the **Royal Monnaie Theatre**. The building in neo-classic style (with very recent extensions) dates from 1819. After a fire gutted the Monnaie theatre on January 21, 1855 a completely new auditorium was built by the architect Poelaert in the most lavish style of the 17th century. Its elliptical shape is somewhat extended by the ceiling.

Nur wenige europäische Opernhäuser können sich einer so glorreichen Vergangenheit und Gegenwart wie die **Königliche Oper "La Monnaie"** rühmen. Das heutige Gebäude wurde, abgesehen von den neuesten Anbauten, im Jahre 1819 im neoklassizistischen Stil erbaut. Nachdem das Théâtre de la Monnaie am 21. Januar 1855 niedergebrannt war, entwarf der Architekt Poelaert einen völlig neuen Saal im prachtvollen Stil des 17. Jh. Er hat die Form einer Ellipse. Diese wird sozusagen bis unter der Decke beibehalten.

Au moyen âge, une petite chapelle s'élevait parmi les potagers à l'extrême limite de la ville, *finis terrae*. Le percement de la rue Neuve fit de l'endroit un quartier commercial qui incita à la construction, au début du XVIIIe siècle, de **l'église Notre-Dame du Finistère** mêlant styles baroque et néo-classique. Récemment restauré, l'intérieur est d'ordonnance classique mais sa décoration est encore franchement baroque.

In de middeleeuwen stond een kleine kapel tussen de moestuintjes aan het uiteinde van de stad, *finis terrae*. De aanleg van de Nieuwstraat maakte van deze omgeving een handelswijk en leidde in het begin van de 18de eeuw tot de constructie van de **Onze-Lieve-Vrouw ter Finisterraekerk**, in een mengeling van barokke en neo-classicistische stijlen. Het interieur werd vrij recent gerestaureerd en is overwegend classicistisch, hoewel de decoratie nog sterk barok is.

In the Middle Ages a little chapel stood among the vegetable gardens at the outer limits of the town, *finis terrae*. When Rue Neuve was laid out a commercial district soon sprang up. This led to the construction at the beginning of the 18th century of the **church of Our Lady of Finistère** in a mixture of baroque and neoclassical styles. The recently restored interior follows the classical order but the decoration is still typically baroque.

Im Mittelalter stand inmitten der Gemüsegärten am äußeren Rand der Stadt, *finis terrae*, eine kleine Kapelle. Der Durchbruch der Rue Neuve verwandelte das Gebiet in ein Handelsviertel, in dem Anfang des 18. Jahrhunderts dann die **Kirche Notre-Dame du Finistère** in einer Mischung aus Barock und Neoklassizismus errichtet wurde. Das kürzlich restaurierte Innere weist eine klassizistische Gestaltung auf, doch die Ausstattung ist noch eindeutig barock.

(À gauche)
La place Rogier n'est plus ce qu'elle était au temps où, chaque jour, la gare du Nord attirait vers elle des milliers de personnes. Un Centre international a remplacé l'ancienne gare de chemins de fer. Mais, la nuit, quand l'éclairage au néon illumine la masse verticale du «**Siru**» (1932), le rêve peut l'emporter sur la réalité. Plusieurs films ont été tournés dans cet hôtel dont la plupart des chambres sont décorées par des artistes belges.

(Ci-dessus et double page suivante)
Longtemps figés dans leur visage ingrat d'avant-guerre, l'**avenue du Boulevard** et le **boulevard Albert II** participent à la renaissance architecturale et urbanistique du quartier. Dans l'optique d'une manière de Manhattan à l'échelle bruxelloise, d'imposants immeubles y ont été érigés.

(Left)
Place Rogier is no longer what it was when the Gare du Nord, now replaced by an international centre, drew thousands of people every day. But at night when neon lights illuminate the vertical mass of "**Siru**" (1932) nostalgia can replace reality. Several films have been shot in this hotel where most of the rooms have been decorated by Belgian artists.

(Above and following double page)
The unattractive pre-war face of the **Avenue du Boulevard** and **Boulevard Albert II** that endured so many years has changed with the architectural and urban renaissance of the district. Imposing buildings have been erected, rather like a mini-Manhattan to the scale of Brussels.

(Links)
Het Rogierplein is niet langer meer de plaats waar dagelijks duizenden mensen langsliepen naar het Noordstation. De halte is nu vervangen door een internationaal centrum. Maar 's nachts kan in de neonverlichting van de verticale massa van de **Siru** (1932) de droom het soms halen van de werkelijkheid. Er werden reeds verscheidene films gedraaid in dit hotel, waarvan de meeste kamers zijn gedecoreerd door Belgische kunstenaars.

(Hierboven en volgende dubbele bladzijde)
De **Bolwerklaan** et de **Albert II laan** hebben jarenlang hun droevig vooroorlogs voorkomen behouden, maar dat veranderde door de bouw- en stedebouwkundige heropleving van de wijk. Er werden imposante torengebouwen neergepoot die Brussel een Manhattan Center op eigen maat gaven.

(Linke Seite)
Die Zeit, in der täglich Tausende vom Rogierplatz zum Nordbahnhof hasteten, ist endgültig vorbei. Ein internationales Zentrum hat die frühere Haltestelle ersetzt. Nachts, wenn das Neonlicht die senkrechten Außenmauem des "**Siru**" (1932) streift, nimmt die Wirklichkeit phantastische Züge an. Viele Zimmer des Hotels wurden von belgischen Künstlern gestaltet, und in manchen wurden Filme gedreht. Was Wunder, wenn dieses Hotel die Reisenden anzieht.

(Oben und folgende Doppelseite)
Avenue du Boulevard und **Boulevard Albert II** boten jahrelang einen trostlosen, an die Zeit vor dem Zweiten Weltkrieg erinnernden Anblick, den sie und das ganze Stadtviertel nun von sich abzuschütteln beginnen. Um ein auf Brüsseler Maßstäbe abgestimmtes Manhattan Center zu errichten, wurden gigantische Hochhäuser gebaut.

Les anciens magasins Waucquez, rue des Sables, furent construits en 1903, à l'âge d'or de Victor Horta qui, après avoir découvert le langage de l'Art Nouveau, s'orientait vers un retour à la tradition. La structure métallique du hall, dont tous les éléments sont de proportions classiques, vise à la transparence qu'accentuent les dalles de verre.

Un moment menacé de destruction, l'édifice parfaitement restauré abrite aujourd'hui le **Centre Belge de la Bande Dessinée**, un art où les dessinateurs belges, depuis Hergé jusqu'à Schuiten et beaucoup d'autres, sont passés maîtres.

Toen Victor Horta in 1903 het voormalige warenhuis Waucquez in de Zandstraat bouwde, was de grondlegger van de Art Nouveau op het toppunt van zijn roem, maar begon hij stilaan terug te grijpen naar meer traditionele bouwvormen. De metalen structuur van de hal, waarvan alle elementen klassieke proporties hebben, streven naar transparantie, wat nog meer in de hand wordt gewerkt door het gebruik van glassteen.

Nadat het dreigde gesloopt te worden, werd het gebouw gerestaureerd en werd er het **Belgische Centrum van het Stripverhaal** geopend, een kunst waarin de Belgische striptekenaars, zoals Hergé, Schuiten en veel anderen, uitblonken.

The former Wauquez stores on Rue des Sables were built in 1903 during the golden age of Victor Horta who, after having digested Art Nouveau, began to return to more traditional styles. The metal framework of the hall with its totally classical proportions aims at luminosity, accentuated by the glass slabs.

Once threatened with destruction, this perfectly restored edifice now serves as the **Comic Strip Centre**, celebrating an art in which Belgians, from Hergé to Schuiten, as well as many others, have long excelled.

1903, als Victor Horta den Jugendstil (Art nouveau) bereits eingeführt hatte und auf der Höhe seines Ruhms stand, begann er wieder, traditionellere Bauformen anzustreben. Das damals entstandene Kaufhaus Waucquez in der Rue des Sables zeigt das sehr deutlich. Die metallenen Bauteile haben klassisch ausgewogene Proportionen und tragen mit den Glasmosaiken zur Überschaubarkeit des Ganzen bei.

Das Gebäude stand auf Abriss, als es restauriert und das **belgische Comiczentrum**, umfunktioniert wurde. Viele belgische Zeichner von Hergé bis Schuiten haben in dieser Branche Hervorragendes geleistet.

△▽

Pour réaliser de 1850 à 1859 la **Colonne du Congrès**, commémorant l'œuvre constitutionnelle du Congrès National convoqué au lendemain de la Révolution de 1830, l'architecte Joseph Poelaert a joué sur les effets de polychromie obtenus grâce à la différence des matériaux : pierre blanche et bleue, bronze, cuivre. Les quatre figures féminines qui entourent le socle représentent les quatre libertés garanties par la Constitution belge (liberté des cultes, d'association, de la presse, d'enseignement). Au pied du monument brûle la flamme du Soldat inconnu.

Onmiddellijk na de omwenteling van 1830 werd het Nationale Congres belast met het maken van de Belgische grondwet. Ter herinnering hieraan werd tussen 1850 en 1859 de **Congreszuil** opgericht. Onder leiding van bouwmeester Jozef Poelaert werden de veelkleurige schakeringen van witachtige stenen en blauwsteen, van brons en van koper tot een indrukwekkend en harmonisch geheel gebundeld. De vier allegorische vrouwengestalten die het voetstuk omringen verzinnebeelden de vier fundamentele vrijheden die door de Belgische Grondwet aan alle burgers gewaarborgd worden (godsdienstvrijheid, vrijheid van vereniging, van onderwijs en persvrijheid). Aan de voet van de gedenkzuil brandt eveneens de vlam ter ere van de onbekende soldaat.

The **Congress Column** commemorating the work of the National Congress summoned after the Revolution of 1830 to draw up the Belgian Constitution was made between 1850-1859 by the architect Joseph Poelaert. The polychrome effect is achieved by the use of various materials – white and greyblue stone, bronze and copper. The four women around the socle symbolize the four freedoms guaranteed by the Constitution (freedom of worship, of association, of the press, of education). The flame of the Unknown Soldier burns at the base of the monument.

Sofort nach dem siegreichen Aufstand von 1830 wurde der Nationale Kongress mit der Ausarbeitung des belgischen Grundgesetzes beauftragt. Um an die vorbildliche Art und Weise zu erinnern, auf die er diesen Auftrag ausführte, wurde diese **Kongresssäule** zwischen 1850 und 1859 errichtet. Es gelang dem Baumeister Joseph Poelaert, die verschiedenen Farbtöne und Reflexe von blauem und weißem Stein, von Bronze und von Kupfer zu einem harmonischen Ganzen zu vereinigen. Die vier weiblichen Gestalten, die den Sockel umringen, stellen die vier Grundfreiheiten dar, welche die belgische Verfassung jedem Bürger sichert (Religions-, Vereins-, Presse- und Unterrichtsfreiheit). Am Fuße der Säule brennt die Flamme zum Andenken an den unbekannten Soldaten.

(Page précédente)
Parmi les hôtels de luxe situés rue Royale, l'**Astoria** a gardé le caractère chaleureux et personnel que lui donne sa décoration de style Louis XVI. Construit un an avant l'Exposition Universelle de 1910, il a été parfaitement rénové. D'illustres personnalités furent les hôtes de l'Astoria : Winston Churchill, Montgomery, Ben Gourion, Giscard d'Estaing, Salvador Dali, Arthur Rubinstein, Peter Ustinov parmi beaucoup d'autres.

(Vorige bladzijde)
Dankzij zijn interieurversiering in Lodewijk XVI-stijl heeft het hotel **Astoria** zijn warme, intieme sfeer beter bewaard dan de andere luxehotels in de Koningsstraat. Het werd voor de wereldtentoonstelling van 1910 gebouwd en vakkundig gerestaureerd. Allerlei beroemdheden waren er te gast, o.a. Winston Churchill, Montgomery, Ben Goerion, Giscard d'Estaing, Salvador Dali, Arthur Rubinstein en Peter Ustinov.

(Preceding page)
Of the luxury hotels on Rue Royale, the **Astoria** has kept the warm and personal character given by its Louis XVI decor. Built shortly before the Universal Exhibition of 1910, it was perfectly restored. Winston Churchill, Montgomery, Ben Gurion, Giscard d'Estaing, Salvador Dali, Arthur Rubinstein and Peter Ustinov are only a few of the many notable guests who have stayed at the Astoria.

(Vorige Seite)
Von den Luxushotels in der Rue Royale hat das Hotel **Astoria** am besten die Wärme und Eigenart bewahrt, die es dem Louis XVI-Stil verdankt. Es wurde für die Weltausstellung von 1910 gebaut und stilgerecht renoviert. Zu seinen Gästen gehörten u.a. Winston Churchill, Montgomery, Ben Gurion, Giscard d'Estaing, Salvador Dali, Arthur Rubinstein und Peter Ustinov.

(Pages 120 à 122)
Les grandes serres et l'orangerie du Jardin Botanique constituent l'une des réussites les plus convaincantes de l'architecture à Bruxelles sous le règne de Guillaume Iᵉʳ de Hollande. L'esplanade et les allées sont ornées d'un remarquable ensemble d'œuvres d'art. Le **Botanique**, repris par l'administration de la Communauté française de Belgique, est devenu un centre culturel très vivant par ses activités théâtrales et ses expositions.

(Bladzijden 120 tot 122)
De grote serres en de oranjerie van de Kruidtuin zijn één van de best geslaagde bouwprogramma's die ten tijde van Willem I van Nederland in Brussel zijn uitgevoerd. De esplanade en de lanen zijn met talrijke en opmerkelijke standbeelden verfraaid. De voormalige serres van de **Botanique** zijn nu het druk bezochte culturele centrum van de Franstalige Gemeenschap waar tentoonstellingen en toneeluitvoeringen plaatshebben.

(Pages 120 to 122)
One of the most successful architectural ensembles in Brussels are the huge greenhouses and orangery of the old Botanical Gardens, built during the reign of William I of Holland. The esplanade and the walks display a remarkable collection of statuary. The **Botanique**, administered by the French speaking community of Belgium, is now a very lively cultural centre, holding theatrical productions and art exhibitions.

(Seiten 120 bis 122)
Die Treibhäuser und die Orangerie des Botanischen Gartens sind eines der gelungensten Bauwerke aus der Zeit (1815-1830), als der niederländische König Wilhelm I. auch über die südlichen Niederlande regierte. Auf dem Vorplatz und den Alleen wurden zahlreiche wertvolle Statuen aufgestellt. Der Gebäudekomplex des **Botanique** ist heute ein sehr reges kulturelles Zentrum, das der französischsprachigen Gemeinschaft gehört und in dem Theateraufführungen und Austellungen einander in rascher Folge ablösen.

▷ Le carrefour du Gros Tilleul à Laeken est dominé par la monumentale **fontaine de Neptune**. Les pieds cernés d'angelots et de sirènes chevauchant des dauphins, le dieu de la mer musclé à souhait semble s'avancer à la conquête de quelque jolie terrestre. Il s'agit, bien sûr, d'une copie de l'original de Jean de Bologne (1529-1608) qui orne la célèbre *Piazza del Nettuno* à Bologne.

Op het kruispunt van de Grote Linde te Laken rijst de indrukwekkende **fontein van Neptunus** op. Aan zijn voeten omringd door engeltjes en op dolfijnen rijdende sirenen, schijnt de forsgebouwde, gespierde zeegod erop uit te gaan een of andere aardse schone te veroveren. Het kunstwerk is een kopie van de fontein die Giambologna (1529-1608) voor de beroemde *Piazza del Nettuno* te Bologna beeldhouwde.

The crossroad of the Gros Tilleul at Laeken is dominated by the huge **fountain of Neptune**. Mermaids perched on dolphins and cherubs cluster around the feet of the brawny sea-god who seems in pursuit of some pretty earthling. The fountain is, of course, a copy of the original by Giambologna (1529-1608) which stands in the famous *Piazza del Nettuno* in Bologna.

An der Strassenkreuzung Gros Tilleul (Dicke Linde) in Laken ragt der wuchtige **Neptunbrunnen** empor. Der muskelstarke Meeresgott, zu dessen Füßen sich Engelchen drängen und Sirenen auf Delphinen herumreiten, eilt, so scheint es, einer schönen Sterblichen entgegen. Es handelt sich natürlich um eine Kopie des Brunnens, den Giambologna (1529-1608) auf der bekannten *Piazza del Nettuno* in Bologna errichtete.

Malgré sa sobriété le **château royal de Laeken** a grande allure au milieu des frondaisons du vaste parc (cent soixante hectares). Rénové après l'incendie du jour de l'an 1890, il a conservé la noblesse de proportion que lui avaient donnée les gouverneurs des Pays-Bas : l'archiduchesse Marie-Christine et le duc de Saxe-Teschen. Napoléon y signa, en 1812, la déclaration de guerre à la Russie.
(Photo panoramique précédente)
En construisant les **serres du château de Laeken** (1874-1893), Alphonse Balat ne réalisa pas seulement un des rêves de Léopold II mais innova en utilisant de façon magistrale la fonte, le fer, l'acier et le verre dans un ensemble architectural. De la serre-perron ou *embarcadère* à l'*église de verre*, ce palais végétal permet de parcourir plus de sept cents mètres parmi les palmiers, les fougères, les plantes tropicales et subtropicales, les camélias et les fleurs de chez nous.
C'est dans le pavillon des palmiers que Léopold II est mort en 1909.

Ondanks zijn soberheid maakt het **Koninklijk Kasteel van Laken**, te midden van het groen van het uitgestrekte park (160 hectare), een grootse indruk. Bij de herstelling na de brand van 1890 werd het evenwicht van de proporties behouden zoals het indertijd gewild was door de gouverneurs der Nederlanden, aartshertogin Maria-Christina en de hertog van Saksen-Teschen. In 1812 ondertekende Napoleon er de oorlogsverklaring aan Rusland.
(Vorige panoramische foto)
Toen Alfons Balat de **serres van het kasteel van Laken** (1874-1893) ontwierp en er op meesterlijke wijze een beroep deed op de architecturale toepassingsmogelijkheden van gietstaal, ijzer, staal en glas, vervulde hij één van de grote dromen van Leopold II. De eerste op een perron of een aanlegsteiger lijkende serre en de laatste, een soort glazen kerk, liggen op meer dan 700 m afstand van elkaar en je wandelt er rond tussen palmbomen, boomvarens, tropische en subtropische planten, camelia's en bloemen uit onze gewesten.
In 1909 overleed Leopold II zelf in de serre met de palmbomen.

The **Royal Château of Laeken** is sober but impressive, standing amid the great trees of its large 160 hectare grounds. Though restored after a fire on New Year's day in 1890, it has not lost the noble proportions which it received from the Austrian governors of the Netherlands, the Archduchess Marie-Christine and the Duke of Saxe-Teschen. It was here that Napoleon signed the declaration of war on Russia in 1812.
(Preceding panoramic photo)
The **greenhouses of the château of Laeken**, built between 1874 and 1893 by Alphonse Balat, according to the wishes of Leopold II are a masterpiece of iron, cast iron, steel and glass. This palace of plants runs 700 metres from the entrance to the glass cathedral through palms, ferns, tropical and sub-tropical plants, camellias and regional flowers.
Leopold II died in the palm greenhouse in 1909.

Trotz seiner Schmucklosigkeit hat das **Königsschloss in Laken** inmitten der Grünanlagen des weiten Parks (160 Hektar) großen Stil. Nach dem Brand am Neujahrstag 1890 renoviert, hat es die edlen Proportionen behalten, die ihm die Statthalter der Niederlande, Erzherzogin Maria-Christina und der Herzog von Sachsen-Teschen gegeben hatten. Napoleon unterschrieb dort 1812 die Kriegserklärung an Russland.
(Voranstehendes Panoramafoto)
Als er die über 700 m langen **Treibhausanlagen im Schlosspark von Laeken** (1874-1893) entwarf, erfüllte Alphonse Balat nicht nur einen Herzenswunsch Leopolds des Zweiten, sondern leistete zugleich Pionierarbeit, indem er die Verwendungsmöglichkeiten von Eisen, Stahl, Gussstahl und Glas auf meisterhafte Weise in sein Baukonzept integrierte.
Im Treibhaus mit den Palmen starb der König Leopold II. 1909.

INGANG JAPANSE TOREN
via Park CHINEES PAVILJOEN

ENTRÉE TOUR JAPONAISE
via Parc PAVILLON CHINOIS

Visitant l'Exposition de Paris en 1900, Léopold II y admira la **Tour japonaise** reconstituée par l'architecte Alexandre Marcel. Après l'exposition, il acheta les plans du bâtiment de quarante mètres de haut et le fit reconstruire à la lisière du domaine royal de Laeken.

Alexandre Marcel se vit également confier par Léopold II la construction d'un **Pavillon chinois**, destiné à l'établissement d'un restaurant de luxe mais qui, faute de concessionnaire, allait devenir unn département des Musées royaux d'Art et d'Histoire. Le kiosque et les boiseries extérieures placées sur trois des façades furent exécutées à Shangaï.

When he visited the 1900 Paris Exhibition, Leopold II greatly admired the **Japanese Tower** constructed by the architect, Alexandre Marcel. When the exhibition ended he bought the plans of the 40 meter high edifice and had it reconstructed on the edge of the royal estate at Laeken.

Leopold II also engaged Alexandre Marcel to construct a **Chinese Pavilion**, supposedly for a deluxe restaurant but which, for lack of a taker, became instead one of the Royal Art and History Museums. The kiosk and the exterior woodwork on three façades were made in Shangai.

Toen hij de wereldtentoonstelling van 1900 te Parijs bezocht, was Leopold II zo verrukt bij het zien van de **Japanse Toren**, dat hij architect Alexander Marcel verzocht de 40 m hoge toren nog eens te bouwen, maar nu aan de rand van het koninklijk domein van Laken.

Leopold II belastte A. Marcel eveneens met de bouw van het **Chinese paviljoen**, dat oorspronkelijk was bedoeld als luxerestaurant. Omdat er na verloop van tijd geen concessiehouder kwam opdagen, is het gebouw een onderdeel van de Koninklijke Musea voor Kunst en Geschiedenis. De kiosk evenals de houten bekleding van de drie gevels werden in Shanghai vervaardigd.

Auf der Weltausstellung in Paris im Jahre 1900 bewunderte Leopold II. den von Alexander Marcel errichteten 40 m hohen **japanischen Turm**, kaufte dem Architekten den Plan ab und ließ den Turm am Rand der königlichen Domäne von Laken wieder aufbauen.

A. Marcel wurde auch von Leopold II. mit der Errichtung des **chinesischen Pavillons** beauftragt, in dem ein Luxusrestaurant vorgesehen war. Seitdem sich kein Konzessionär mehr meldet, dient der Pavillon als Zweigstelle der Königlichen Museen für Kunst und Geschichte. Der Kiosk und die an den drei Fassaden angebrachten Holzverkleidungen wurden in Schanghai angefertigt.

▷

Le 16 juin 1550 fut donné le premier coup de pelle pour le creusement du canal de Willebroek reliant Bruxelles au Rupel et, de là, à l'Escaut et la mer. De grandes festivités célébrèrent son ouverture au trafic en 1561. Le raccordement au canal de Charleroi, creusé en 1827, puis l'élargissement du canal maritime permirent le rapide développement d'un port intérieur comportant des bassins et accessible aux navires de moyen tirant d'eau. Environ six millions de tonnes de marchandises sont débarqués et embarqués chaque année au **port de Bruxelles**.

Op 16 juni 1550 werd de eerste spadesteek gegeven voor het graven van het kanaal van Willebroek, dat Brussel verbindt met de Rupel en vandaar met de Schelde en de zee. De openstelling voor de scheepvaart in 1561 werd met grote festiviteiten gevierd. De verbinding met het kanaal Brussel-Charleroi die in 1827 werd gegraven, en later de verbreding van het zeekanaal, bevorderden de snelle groei van een binnenhaven met dokken, die toegankelijk is voor schepen met een gemiddelde diepgang. Ongeveer zes miljoen ton goederen worden jaarlijks gelost en geladen in de **haven van Brussel**.

On June 16, 1550 the first shovel began to dig the canal of Willebroek which would link Brussels to Rupel and from there to the Scheldt and the sea. Great festivities were held when it opened to traffic in 1561. It was linked to the Charleroi canal in 1827 and then the maritime canal was enlarged, permitting the rapid development of an inland port with basins accessible to ships of medium draft. About six million tonnes of goods are embarked and unloaded annually in the **port of Brussels**.

Am 16. Juni 1550 erfolgte der erste Spatenstich für den Aushub des Kanals von Willebroek, der Brüssel mit Rupel und weiter mit der Schelde und dem Meer verbinden sollte. Dessen Freigabe für den Verkehr im Jahre 1561 wurde mit einem großen Fest begangen. Der 1827 geschaffene Anschluss an den Kanal von Charleroi und später die Erweiterung des Meereskanals ermöglichten die schnelle Entwicklung eines mehrere Becken umfassenden und für Schiffe mit mittlerem Tiefgang zugänglichen Binnenhafens. Rund sechs Millionen Tonnen Güter werden jährlich im **Hafen von Brüssel** umgeschlagen.

△
Dans les vitres du *Trade Mart* voisin se reflète l'**Atomium**, érigé à l'occasion de l'Exposition Universelle de 1958. Il n'était pas destiné à lui survivre longtemps, mais sa construction s'avéra très résistante. Aussi bien, ses neuf sphères couvertes d'aluminium brillent toujours sur le plateau du Heysel. Reliées par des tubes d'acier, elles figurent une molécule de cristal de fer agrandie 165 milliards de fois.

Het **Atomium**, dat ter gelegenheid van de wereldtentoonstelling van 1958 gebouwd werd, weerspiegelt zich in de ramen van de *Trade Mart*. Alhoewel dat aanvankelijk niet voorzien was, trotseerde het stevige gevaarte de tand des tijds, zodat de negen met aluminiumplaten bedekte bollen nog altijd boven het Heizelplateau staan te glanzen. Samen met de buizen die ze met elkaar verbinden, vormen ze een 165 miljard maal vergrote ijzerkristalmolecule.

The **Atomium**, erected for the Universal Exhibition of 1958, is reflected in the windows of the neighbouring *"Trade Mart"*. Though it was not meant to endure for such a long time, it was very well constructed and so its nine spheres continue to to sparkle on the Heysel plateau. Linked by steel tubes they form an iron crystal molecule enlarged 165 billion times.

In den Fenstern des *Trade Mart* spiegelt sich das **Atomium**, das anlässlich der Weltausstellung von 1958 gebaut wurde. Obschon dies anfänglich nicht geplant war, glänzen die neun mit Aluminiumplatten bedeckten Kugeln der wetterfesten Konstruktion noch immer über dem Heysel. Die Kugeln mit den sie verbindenden Röhren sind die Abbildung eines 165 milliardenfach vergrößerten Eisenkristallmoleküls.

△

Sur les conseils de saint Thomas d'Aquin avec qui elle correspondait, la duchesse Aleyde, veuve de Henri III de Brabant, fonda en 1262 un couvent de sœurs dominicaines auquel elle donna le nom de Val Duchesse. Le domaine du **Val Duchesse** (boulevard du Souverain) participe pleinement à la vie de l'Union Européenne en accueillant nos hôtes étrangers lors d'assemblées officielles et en leur offrant un centre de rencontres privées.

Op aanbeveling van de heilige Thomas Van Aquino, met wie zij correspondeerde, stichtte hertogin Aleydis, de weduwe van Hendrik III van Brabant, in 1262 een klooster voor Dominicanessen, dat zij Hertoginnendal noemde. Het domein van **Hertoginnendal** aan de Vorstlaan vormt vaak het decor voor de activiteiten van de Europese Gemeenschap: buitenlandse gasten worden hier bij officiële bijeenkomsten ontvangen en hebben tevens de ruimte voor privé-ontmoetingen.

In the year 1262, acting on the advice of St. Thomas Aquinas with whom she was in correspondence, Duchess Aleyde, the widow of Henri III of Brabant, founded a convent of Dominican nuns which she named Val Duchesse. The **Val Duchesse** estate (Boulevard du Souverain) is now closely associated with the life of the European Community, being the reception point for foreign guests who come to Brussels for official discussions, and providing them with an ideal setting for private talks.

Auf Anraten des Hl. Thomas von Aquin, mit dem sie im Briefwechsel stand, gründete die Herzogin Aleyde, Witwe Heinrichs III. von Brabant, 1262 ein Dominikanerinnenkloster, dem sie den Namen Val Duchesse gab. Heute ist die Domaine **Val Duchesse** am Boulevard du Souverain Zeuge des aktiven Lebens der Europäischen Gemeinschaft: Sie dient dem Empfang hoher ausländischer Gäste anlässlich offizieller Sitzungen oder privater Gespräche bzw. Zusammenkünfte.

▷

Se mirant gracieusement dans un étang, le **château Malou** (boulevard de la Woluwe) a l'allure apaisante des manoirs du XVIIIᵉ siècle. Fort opportunément, les édiles de Woluwe-Saint-Lambert l'ont affecté à de multiples activités culturelles, dont la plus originale est peut-être un service de prêt d'œuvres d'art contemporain.

Het **kasteel Malou** aan de Woluwelaan weerspiegelt in een slotvijver de rustige zelfzekerheid der versterkte woonsten uit de 18de eeuw. De gemeenteraad van Sint-Lambrechts-Woluwe heeft een gelukkig initiatief genomen door het open te stellen voor talrijke culturele manifestaties waarvan de origineelste misschien wel de uitleendienst van hedendaagse kunstwerken is.

Mirrored gracefully in its pond, the **Malou mansion** (Boulevard de la Woluwe) has the peaceful appearance of an 18th century manor house. The local authorities of Woluwe-Saint-Lambert wisely decided that it should be used for cultural purposes, the most original of which is a loan service of contemporary art.

Das sich am Boulevard de la Woluwe verträumt in einem Weiher spiegelnde **Schloss Malou** besitzt die stille Anmut der Herrensitze aus dem 18. Jh. Die Gemeindeväter von Woluwe-Saint-Lambert haben es ganz zweckmäßig in ein Zentrum für kulturelle Veranstaltungen umfunktioniert und dort u.a. eine in ihrer Art einmalige Leihstelle für moderne Gemälde angesiedelt.

△
Fondé par un chapelain de Sainte-Gudule et un ermite, le **Rouge-Cloître** doit son nom au mortier fait de tuiles pilées qui enduisait ses murs au XIVᵉ siècle. Les chanoines de Saint-Augustin firent du Rouge-Cloître un des prieurés les plus rayonnants du Brabant. Un long corps de logis, des pans de muraille, une porte sommée d'un blason et des étangs, voilà tout ce qui subsiste, à Auderghem, du monastère où le peintre Hugo van der Goes, frère convers, mourut halluciné en 1482 à l'âge de quarante-deux ans.

Het **Rood Klooster** werd gesticht door een kanunnik van Sint-Goedele en een kluizenaar. De abdij heeft haar naam te danken aan het feit dat de monniken in de 14de eeuw, om de omheining waterdicht te maken, haar met specie van gestampte dakpannen hadden bestreken. De kanunniken van Sint-Augustinus maakten het Rood Klooster tot één der schitterendste priorijen van Brabant. Een lang hoofdgebouw, muurpanden, een poort getopt door een wapenschild en vijvers zijn al wat overblijft van dit klooster in Oudergem, waarin de krankzinnig geworden kunstschilder en lekenbroeder Hugo van der Goes in 1482 op 42-jarige leeftijd stierf.

Founded by a chaplain of Saint Gudule and a hermit, **Rouge-Cloître** owes its name to the mortar, made of crushed tiles, with which its walls were covered in the 14th century. The canons of Saint Augustine made Rouge-Cloître into one of the most influential priories in Brabant. A long main wing, remnants of wall, a door bearing a crest, and some ponds are all that remains of the monastery in Auderghem where the painter Hugo van der Goes, a lay brother, died in a state of hallucination in 1482, at the age of 42.

Von einem Einsiedler und einem Kaplan der Gudulakirche gegründet, verdankt **Rouge-Cloître** (das rote Kloster) dem Mörtel aus gestoßenen Ziegelsteinen, mit dem seine Mauern im 14. Jh. bestrichen waren, seinen Namen. Die Stiftsherren des heiligen Augustinus machten aus dem Rouge-Cloître eine der strahlendsten Propstein Brabants. Ein langes Hauptgebäude, Mauerreste, ein Tor mit einem Wappen und Teiche sind alles, was von dem Kloster in Auderghem übrig bleibt, in dem der Maler Hugo van des Goes, ein Laienbruder, 1482 im Alter von 42 Jahren im Fieberwahn starb.

Les paroissiens de **Saint-Clément à Watermael** sont privilégiés. Ils conservent depuis le XIᵉ siècle une église villageoise romane. À l'origine, la tour qui servait de refuge n'était accessible que par une échelle et l'on pénétrait dans le sanctuaire par une porte latérale.

De parochianen van de **St.-Clemenskerk te Watermaal** zijn bevoorrecht. Zij bezitten een Romaanse dorpskerk uit de 11de eeuw. Oorspronkelijk was de toren, die dienst deed als wijkplaats, slechts via een ladder toegankelijk en ging men het heiligdom binnen langs een zij-deur.

The parishioners of **Saint Clement at Watermael** are a privileged community. Since the 11th century, they have been able to keep their Romanesque village church. Originally the tower – which was used as a refuge – could only be reached by a ladder, and the church was entered by a side-door.

Die Pfarrkinder von **St.-Clement in Watermaal** besitzen seit dem 11. Jh. eine schöne romanische Dorfkirche. Ursprünglich war der Turm – der als Zufluchtsort diente – nur mittels einer Leiter zugänglich, und man trat durch eine Seitentür in die Kirche ein.

Au temps de Charles Quint, la **forêt de Soignes** s'étendait sur plus de dix mille hectares. Aujourd'hui, sa superficie se trouve réduite de moitié, ce qui est encore considérable aux portes d'une capitale. Depuis le moyen âge, elle abritait de nombreux prieurés et abbayes, où chanoines augustins et moines vivaient dans le recueillement et le travail: Rouge-Cloître où mourut Hugo van der Goes, Groenendael où vécut le grand mystique Jan Van Ruisbroeck, Forest, la Cambre, Val Duchesse. En 1815, malgré de considérables défrichements, la forêt de Soignes cernait encore le village de Waterloo. Mais à la fin de 1822, lors de la création de la «Société Générale des Pays-Bas pour le Développement de l'Industrie», le roi Guillaume Ier fit l'apport de biens immobiliers estimés à vingt millions de florins, notamment la forêt de Soignes; il reçut en contrepartie cinq cent mille florins par an. La «Société Générale» pouvait aliéner ses biens, sauf un tiers de la forêt de Soignes. En fait, loin d'aliéner, elle fit d'excellentes acquisitions. En 1843, elle céda la forêt de Soignes à l'Etat belge pour seize millions et demi de florins.

Ten tijde van Karel de Vijfde had het **Zoniënwoud** een oppervlakte van meer dan 10.000 hectare. Al is die nu tot op de helft verminderd, het blijft indrukwekkend, vooral vlak bij een hoofdstad. Sedert de Middeleeuwen was het bezaaid met priorijen en abdijen waar augustijner kanunniken en monniken een evenwicht tussen contemplatie en bedrijvigheid trachtten te vinden: het Rood Klooster, waar Hugo van der Goes overleed, Groenendaal, waar de grote mysticus Jan van Ruisbroeck vertoefde, Ter Kameren, Vorst, Hertoginnendal. Alle ontbossingen ten spijt omsloot het Zoniënwoud het dorpje Waterloo in 1815 nog aan alle kanten. Op het einde van 1822 ontstond de "Generale Maatschappij der Nederlanden voor de Ontwikkeling van de Nijverheid", waarvoor koning Willem I der Nederlanden onroerende goederen ter waarde van 20 miljoen gulden, o.a. het Zoniënwoud, bijdroeg. In ruil daarvoor kreeg hij 500.000 gulden per jaar. De "Generale Maatschappij" mocht haar bezit vervreemden op een derde van het Zoniënwoud na. In feite slaagde ze erin door aankoop nieuwe gronden te verwerven, maar in 1843 verkocht ze het Zoniënwoud voor 16,5 miljoen gulden aan de Belgische Staat.

During the reign of Charles V the **Soignes Forest** covered more than 10,000 hectares. The present forest is half that size but still very large for a forest touching a capital city. In the Middle Ages there were many priories and abbeys where Augustinian monks lived and worked, withdrawn from the world : Rouge-Cloître where Hugo van der Goes died, Groenendael where the great mystic Blessed Jan van Ruysbroeck lived, Forest, La Cambre and Val-Duchesse. In 1815 the Soignes Forest still encircled the village of Waterloo, despite much clearing. At the end of 1822 when the "Société Générale des Pays-Bas pour le Développement de l'Industrie" was formed King William I contributed real estate estimated at 20 million florins, the Soignes Forest providing a large part of the investment. The King received 500,000 florins annually in return. The "Société Générale" could dispose of its holdings, except for a third of the forest. In fact, instead of selling it off, it made some excellent acquisitions and in 1843 the company sold the Soignes Forest to the Belgian state for sixteen and a half million florins.

Zur Zeit Karls des Fünften war der **Sonienwald** ein 10.000 ha großer Buchenwald. Obwohl er nun noch kaum halb so groß ist, mutet er immer noch wie eine Himmelsgabe vor den Pforten einer Hauptstadt an. Im Mittelalter wurden dort Prioreien und Abteien gegründet, in denen Augustinermönche und Chorherren einem teils beschaulichen, teils aktiven Leben oblagen: Das "Rote Kloster" (Rouge-Cloître), in dem Hugo van der Goes starb, Groenendael, wo der große Mystiker Jan van Ruisbroeck lebte, Forest, La Cambre, Val Duchesse. 1815 umschloss der Wald die Ortschaft Waterloo noch von allen Seiten. Ende 1822 entstand die "Gemeinnützige Gesellschaft der Niederlande zur Förderung der Industrie" zu der König Wilhelm der Niederlande Grundbesitz im Werte von 20 Millionen Gulden, u.a. den Sonienwald, beisteuerte, wofür ihm jährlich 500.000 Gulden ausgezahlt wurden. Abgesehen von einem Drittel des Sonienwaldes durfte die Gesellschaft ihren Grundbesitz abstoßen. Sie tat jedoch das Gegenteil und trat dann 1843 den Sonienwald für 16,5 Millionen an den belgischen Staat ab.

Joliment vallonné, le **Bois de la Cambre** a été dessiné par l'architecte de jardins Keilig. Il fait agréablement alterner les pelouses et les futaies. Aubaine pour les citadins, il s'ouvre à l'extrémité de l'avenue Louise et s'allonge sur environ deux kilomètres.

Tuinarchitect Keilig ontwierp het **Ter Kamerenbos** met zijn zachte glooiingen. De wisselbouw van bomengroepen en grasmatten is een genot voor het oog en een groene long voor de stedelingen. De Louizalaan eindigt op dit bos dat zich uitstrekt over ongeveer twee kilometer.

The gentle slopes of the **La Cambre Wood** were designed by the garden architect Keilig. Lawns alternate with trees and thickets. City dwellers in Brussels are fortunate to have this wood at the end of the Avenue Louise, from whence it stretches some two kilometres.

Der **Bois de la Cambre** genannte Park mit seinen sanften Hügeln wurde vom Gartenarchitekten Keilig entworfen. Rasenplätze und Waldflächen lösen einander aufs angenehmste ab. Dieser Park, den die Brüsseler wie eine Himmelsgabe zu schätzen wissen, dehnt sich vom Ende der Avenue Louise etwa zwei Kilometer weit aus.

△▷

Fondée à la fin du XIIIe siècle par des religieuses cisterciennes, l'**abbaye de la Cambre** fut dévastée par les calvinistes et les Espagnols sous le règne troublé de Philippe II d'Espagne. Ce n'est qu'au XVIIIe siècle que les abbesses purent édifier de nouveaux bâtiments conventuels dans le style Louis XV. L'église gothique date de la seconde moitié du XIVe siècle. Les colonnes, chapiteaux corinthiens, niches et fronton du porche furent conçus pour assurer la liaison avec les constructions qui forment la cour d'honneur, notamment l'élégant palais abbatial.

Une partie de l'ancienne abbaye, dans la commune d'Auderghem, est actuellement occupée par l'importante École nationale des Arts visuels.

The **Abbey of La Cambre** founded at the end of the 13th century by Cistercian nuns was ruined by the Calvinists and the Spanish during the turbulent reign of Philip II of Spain. It was only in the 18th that the Abbesses could build new conventual buildings in the Louis XV style. The columns, Corinthian capitals, niches and pediment of the porch were designed to harmonize with the buildings forming the great courtyard, notably the elegant abbatial palace.

A part of the abbey, in the municipality of Auderghem, is presently occupied by the prestigious National School of the visual Arts.

De **abdij Ter Kameren** werd op het einde van de 13de eeuw gesticht door cisterciënzers. Onder het woelige bewind van Filips II van Spanje werd de abdij verwoest door calvinisten en Spanjaarden. Pas in de 18de eeuw konden de abdissen nieuwe kloostergebouwen oprichten in Lodewijk XV-stijl. De gotische kerk dateert van de tweede helft van de 14de eeuw. De zuilen, corintische kapitelen, nissen en frontons van het kerkportaal vormen een verbinding met de gebouwen van het voorplein, waaronder het elegante abdijpaleis.

Een deel van de oude abdij, in de gemeente Oudergem, is momenteel in gebruik genomen door de belangrijke nationale School voor Visuele Kunsten.

Die Ende des 13. Jahrhunderts von den Zisterzienserinnen gegründete **Abtei La Cambre** wurde von den Kalvinisten und den Spaniern während der unruhigen Herrscherzeit Philips II. von Spanien verwüstet. Erst im 18. Jahrhundert konnten die Äbtissinnen neue Klostergebäude im Louis-quinze-Stil errichten. Die gotische Kirche stammt aus der zweiten Hälfte des 14. Jahrhunderts. Die Säulen, die korinthischen Kapitelle, die Nischen und der Frontgiebel des Portalvorbaus wurden zur Verbindung mit den Anlagen des Ehrenhofs, insbesondere dem eleganten Abteipalais, geschaffen.

Ein Teil der alten Abtei in der Gemeinde Auderghem beherbergt derzeit die bedeutende Staatliche Schule für visuelle Künste.

Le premier **Observatoire**, établi en ville près de la porte de Schaerbeek et longtemps dirigé par Adolphe Quételet, s'est avéré trop exigu et gêné par le bruit et les variations de température. L'institution fut transférée en 1890 à Uccle, au sein d'un vaste parc circulaire situé à cent deux mètres d'altitude.

(Page de droite)
Créé peu après l'hécatombe de 1866 due à une épidémie de choléra, le **cimetière du Dieweg à Uccle** vit se multiplier les tombes israélites à partir de 1877. Le champ de repos israélite de Saint-Gilles était alors saturé et dut être désaffecté. L'absence de décor figuré caractérise la plupart des tombeaux juifs. D'où l'édification de monuments funéraires qui, par leur architecture, s'apparentent à de petits temples antiques, témoignant de la richesse de nombreuses familles, dont beaucoup furent tragiquement éteintes ou dispersées pendant la Seconde Guerre mondiale.

(Hierboven)
De eerste **Sterrenwacht**, die lange tijd onder leiding stond van Adolphe Quételet, was gevestigd in het centrum van Brussel, bij de Schaarbeekse Poort. Door plaatsgebrek, lawaai en temperatuurschommelingen werd het instituut in 1890 overgeplaatst naar Ukkel, waar het gelegen is in een groot rond park, 102 meter boven de zeespiegel.

(Rechterbladzijde)
Omwille van het fel stijgend dodenaantal tijdens de cholera-epidemie van 1866 werd er een nieuw **kerkhof aan de Dieweg in Ukkel** aangelegd. De joodse graven werden er al maar talrijker, nadat het overvolle Israëlische kerkhof van Sint-Gillis in 1877 buiten dienst was gesteld. Er ontbreekt op de joodse graven meestal elke vorm van figuratieve uitbeelding. Daarom lijken veel van die grafmonumenten in bouwkundig opzicht op antieke tempeltjes, vooral die van de talrijke welgestelde families. Hun nakomelingen werden tijdens de tweede wereldoorlog vaak op tragische wijze uitgemoord of verdreven.

(Above)
The first **Observatory** was situated in town near the Schaerbeek gate and was directed for many years by Adolphe Quételet. It became too cramped and the noise and variations in temperature made work there very difficult. The observatory was relocated to Uccle in 1890, set in a large circular park at an altitude of 102 meters.

(Page Right)
The **Dieweg Cemetery in Uccle** was established shortly after the great cholera epidemic of 1866. After 1877 more and more Jewish people were buried there as the Jewish cemetery at St. Gilles was full and could no longer be used. Most of the Jewish tombs are not decorated. As if to compensate for this are the many tombs built to look like small, antique temples, attesting to the wealth of a large number of families. It is tragic that a great many of these families were extinguished or scattered during the Second World War.

(Oben)
Die erste **Wetter- und Sternwarte** befand sich im Stadtzentrum bei der Porte de Schaerbeek und wurde jahrelang von Adolphe Quételet geleitet. Platzmangel, Lärm und Temperaturunterschiede führten 1890 zum Umzug nach Uccle, in einen großen, runden Park, der 102 m über dem Meeresspiegel liegt.

(Rechte Seite)
Als 1866 eine Choleraepidemie viele Menschen dahinraffte, entstand ein neuer **Friedhof am Dieweg in Uccle**. Auch die Zahl der Juden, die dort ihre letzte Ruhestätte fanden, nahm zu, vor allem weil der jüdische Friedhof von Saint-Gilles ab 1877 wegen Platzmangels nicht mehr zur Verfügung stand. Viele jüdischen Grabmäler gleichen antiken Tempelchen, vor allem die der wohlhabenden Familien, deren Nachkommen leider größtenteils während des Zweiten Weltkriegs ermordet oder vertrieben wurden.

Édifiée en 1893, la **maison Tassel** (rue Paul-Emile Janson) est l'une des premières demeures privées que Victor Horta a conçues dans le style Art Nouveau qui, à l'époque, fit sensation, voire scandale.

(Ci-dessus)
À l'âge de quarante ans, parvenu à une enviable célébrité, Victor Horta décida de s'offrir, rue Américaine, une demeure et des bureaux où il pourrait donner libre cours à son talent et à son imagination. Les deux bâtiments, construits en 1898, se différencient assez fort. Dès l'entrée de ce qui est aujourd'hui le **musée Victor Horta**, s'offrent aux regards du visiteur toute la richesse d'une conception spatiale propre à l'Art Nouveau, toute la chaleur des peintures dans les tons orangés et toute la finesse des ferronneries. Les meubles qui occupent les salons et la salle à manger sont tous conçus par Victor Horta.

(Page right)
The **Tassel house** on Rue Paul-Emile Janson was one of the first private residences designed by Victor Horta in 1893 in the then new Art Nouveau style considered sensational, if not scandalous, at that time.

(Above)
At the age of forty Victor Horta, recognized as a highly reputed architect, decided to build himself a home and offices on Rue Américaine which would display the range of his talent and imagination. The two buildings, built in 1898, are quite different. As soon as the visitor enters what is now the **Victor Horta Museum**, the originality of the Art Nouveau conception of space, the warmth of the orange-toned paint and the elegance of the ironwork become evident. The furniture in the reception rooms and the dining room was all designed by Victor Horta.

(Rechterbladzijde)
Het in 1893 gebouwde **herenhuis Tassel** in de Paul-Emiel Jansonstraat is één van de eerste privéwoningen die Victor Horta in Art Nouveaustijl optrok. Een stijl die toen nog voor opschudding en zelfs schandaal zorgde.

(Hierboven)
Op veertigjarige leeftijd besloot de toen al beroemde architect Victor Horta in de Amerikaansestraat een eigen huis met kantoorruimten te bouwen. Bij het ontwerpen ervan liet hij zijn talent en verbeelding vrij spel. De twee in 1898 opgetrokken gebouwen zijn nogal verschillend. Bij het betreden van het huidige **Victor Hortamuseum** wordt de bezoeker al dadelijk geconfronteerd met de grote vindingrijkheid van de Art Nouveau wat betreft volumeschepping, kleurschakering met dominerende warme oranjetinten en het verfijnde vormenspel van het smeedwerk. Ook alle meubels in de woon- en eetkamer zijn door Horta zelf ontworpen.

(Rechte Seite)
Das 1893 gebaute herrschaftliche **Haus Tassel** in der Rue Paul-Emile Janson ist eines der ersten Privathäuser, die Victor Horta in seiner damals noch Aufsehen, ja sogar Entrüstung erregenden Variante des Jugendstils errichtete.

(Oben)
Im Alter von vierzig Jahren beschloss der bereits berühmte Architekt Victor Horta, sich in der Rue Américaine ein Haus mit Atelier und Büroräumen zu bauen. Dabei ließ er seinem erfinderischen Talent freien Lauf. Die beiden 1898 errichteten Gebäude sind recht verschieden. Bereits am Eingang tritt dem Besucher des heutigen **Victor Horta Museums** der ganze erfinderische Reichtum des Jugendstils entgegen: das neue Raumgefühl, die originelle, warme, orangegelbe Töne bevorzugende Farbgebung, die erlesene Eleganz des Schmiedewerks. Alle in Ess- und Wohnzimmer aufgestellten Möbel wurden nach sehr genauen Entwürfen Victor Hortas hergestellt.

En concevant les plans de la **prison de Saint-Gilles** (1878-1884), implantée au cœur de cette commune urbaine, les architectes se sont inspirés des redoutables forteresses médiévales. Le mur d'enceinte et les tours crénelés étaient visiblement destinés tant à dissuader les prisonniers de toute tentative d'évasion qu'à convaincre le passant de la force invincible de la justice répressive.

Bij de opmaak van de plannen voor de **gevangenis van Sint-Gillis** (1878-1884), die middenin deze stadswijk staat, lieten de architecten zich inspireren door de ontzagwekkende middeleeuwse burchten. De omwallingsmuur en de torens met kantelen waren duidelijk bedoeld om zowel de gevangenen elke poging tot ontsnapping te ontraden als de voorbijgangers te overtuigen van de onoverwinnelijke kracht van de rechtspraak.

When drawing up the plans for the **Saint-Gilles' prison** (1878-1884), situated in the heart of this urban municipality, the architects were inspired by formidable mediæval fortresses. The walls with their crenelated towers were just as much aimed at convincing not only the prisoners but those passing by of the invincible power of repressive justice.

Bei der Ausarbeitung der Pläne für das **Gefängnis von Saint-Gilles** (1878-1884) im Herzen dieser Stadtgemeinde ließen sich die Architekten von den furchterregenden mittelalterlichen Festungen inspirieren. Die Umfassungs-mauer und die zinnenbewehrten Türme waren ganz offensichtlich dazu bestimmt, einerseits die Häftlinge von jeglichem Fluchversuch abzuschrecken, und andererseits die Passanten von der unüberwindbaren Stärke der Strafanstalt zu überzeugen.

L'**église Saints-Pierre-et-Guidon**
d'Anderlecht, dont la fondation
remonterait à l'an 800, fut édifiée du
XIVᵉ au XVIᵉ siècle mais ne vit l'achèvement de sa flèche qu'en 1898.
(Pages 149 et 150)
Un jardin sépare l'église de la pai-
sible **maison dite d'Erasme**, rue du
Chapitre à Anderlecht. L'auteur de
l'«Eloge de la Folie» s'y installa du
mois de mai à la fin d'octobre 1521,
pendant que se construisait la tour de
la collégiale. Erasme aimait beaucoup
Bruxelles, sans doute parce que cette
ville semble vouée au rôle d'arbitre et
de conciliateur, le rôle qu'il voulut
jouer jusqu'à son dernier souffle.

De **St.-Pieter en St.-Guidokerk** te
Anderlecht, die in 800 gesticht zou
zijn, werd opgericht van de 14de tot
de 16de eeuw. De bouw van de torenspits werd evenwel pas in 1898 voltooid.
(Blz. 149 en 150)
Het zg. **Erasmushuis** in de
Kapittelstraat te Anderlecht, waarin
de auteur van "Het Lof der Zotheid"
van mei tot einde oktober 1521 vertoefde, is door een tuin gescheiden van
de kerk, waarvan de toren in die tijd
werd opgetrokken. Erasmus hield
ongetwijfeld veel van Brussel, de stad
waaraan ook herhaaldelijk de verzoe-
nende, scheidsrechterlijke rol was toe-
bedeeld, een rol die hijzelf tot zijn laatste snik speelde.

The **church of Saints Peter and
Guidon** at Anderlecht, believed to
have been founded in the year 800,
was built between the 14th and 16th
century, but the spire was only completed in 1898.
(Pages 149 and 150)
A garden separates the church from
the peaceful **Erasmus house** on Rue
du Chapitre in Anderlecht. The author
of "The Praise of Folly" stayed there
from May to October of 1521 while
the tower of the collegiate church was
being built. Erasmus was very fond of
Brussels, perhaps because the city
seemed to him as dedicated to the task
of arbitration and conciliation as he
was himself until his death.

Die **St.-Peter-und-Guido Kirche**
in Anderlecht, deren Gründung auf
das Jahr 800 zurückgehen soll, wurde
vom 14.-16. Jh. errichtet, aber ihre
Turmspitze wurde erst 1898
vollendet.
(Seiten 149 und 150)
Die Kirche ist durch einen Garten
vom stillen **Erasmus-Haus** in der Rue
du Chapitre in Anderlecht getrennt, in
dem der Autor des "Lobes der
Narrheit" von Mai bis Ende Oktober
1521 verweilte, gerade als der Turm
der Stiftskirche errichtet wurde.
Erasmus wohnte gern in Brüssel,
gewiss weil dieser Stadt auch damals
schon die Rolle des beschwichtigenden
Schiedsrichters eigen war, die er selber
bis zu seinem letzten Atemzuge zu
spielen gewillt war.

VINCENT MERCKX
EDITIONS

www.merckxeditions.com

© 2003 Editions Merckx Uitgeverij s.p.r.l. b.v.b.a.
Avenue des Statuaires 145A Beeldhouwerslaan, B-1180 Bruxelles Brussel
☎ +32/2/374.41.56 • Fax +32/2/375.80.37

Photographs
Vincent Merckx

Photoassistant
Philippe Molitor

Texts
Georges-Henri Dumont

Nederlandse bewerking & Deutsche Übersetzung
DSDB

English translation
Sheila Tessier-Lavigne

Typesetting
Deloge

Printing
Daneels Group

D-2000-0398-24
ISBN 90-74847-24-2

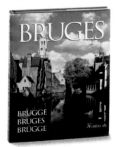